Caring School Community™

Homeside Activities

Activities
That Connect
Home and School

Grade 5

**DEVELOPMENTAL
STUDIES CENTER™**

Acknowledgments

Homeside Activities are the product of many people—thousands of parents, teachers, and children in San Ramon, Hayward, San Francisco, Cupertino, and Salinas, California; Louisville, Kentucky; Miami and Homestead, Florida; and White Plains, New York, who piloted them.

Copyright © Developmental Studies Center

Developmental Studies Center
2000 Embarcadero, Suite 305
Oakland, CA 94606-5300
(800) 666-7270, fax: (510) 464-3670
www.devstu.org

ISBN-13: 978-1-57621-545-6
ISBN-10: 1-57621-545-8

Printed in the United States of America

 2 3 4 5 6 7 8 9 10

A Simple Parent-Teacher Partnership for Kids

No matter who you ask, you won't get an argument about whether parents should be involved in their children's education—but you won't get many suggestions for a simple, inclusive way to make it happen, either. That's why Homeside Activities are so powerful. They provide a low-key, nonthreatening way for teachers and parents to build partnerships for kids.

These short, concrete activities in English and Spanish foster communication between teachers and parents and between parents and children. They make it easy for parents to contribute a "homeside" to their children's schoolside learning. And they make it easy for children to "schedule" personal time with a parent or other caretaking adult.

Implicit in the design of Homeside Activities is a message of respect for the diversity of children's families and communities. All activities build on the value for parents and children of talking with each other and listening to each other—in their home language. The activities recognize the social capital of the relationships children go home to when the dismissal bell rings every day. It's important for children to know that the adults guiding them at home are valued by the adults guiding them at school.

Homeside Activities are introduced once or twice a month in class, completed at home, and then incorporated into a follow-up classroom activity or discussion. Typically these 15- to 20-minute activities are reciprocal parent-child interviews or opportunities to share experiences and opinions. The activities are organized by grade level, but none of them have grade-specific references; they can also be used in mixed-grade and ungraded classrooms. The activity topics relate to academic, social, or citizenship themes that are integral to the life of almost any classroom.

For example, in a "Family Folklore" activity for fifth-graders, children learn about their own history while they collect family stories at home; then they contribute to the classroom community by sharing some of these stories in class. One classroom using this activity learned about a runaway slave who lived among the Seminoles, a courtship in which a borrowed Lincoln Continental became a neighborhood attraction, and an extended-family band that serves up the entertainment for family weddings. These seemingly small pieces of information make a big difference in how children and teachers view each other in the classroom.

BENEFITS OF HOMESIDE ACTIVITIES

	FOR STUDENTS	FOR TEACHERS	FOR PARENTS

Academic/ Intellectual	• chance to "schedule" time with parent or other adult
	• build commitment to learning
	   - engage interest of parent
	   - see importance and relevance of learning to adult life
	• build literacy
	   - communicate clearly
	   - compare information
	   - compare points of view
	   - think abstractly
	• rehearse school learning
	• reinforce school learning
	• reinforce value of home language
		• students more invested in academics because of adult involvement
		• more ways to connect new learning for students
		   - more aware of students' experiences
		   - more aware of students' knowledge
		• opportunity to inform parents of classroom learning program
		• opportunity to encourage use of home language
			• fail-safe way to contribute to child's school learning
			• exposure to classroom learning approach
			• exposure to classroom learning topics
			• opportunity to enjoy child's thinking
			• opportunity to reinforce importance and relevance of learning
			• opportunity to reinforce value of home language

Citizenship	• chance to "schedule" time with parent or other adult
	• build commitment to values
	   - engage interest of parent
	   - see importance and relevance of values to adult life
	• build complex understanding of values
	   - compare information
	   - compare points of view
	   - think abstractly
	• reinforce school learning
		• students more conscious of values
		• students more open to examining their behavior
		• students more likely to see similarities between home and school values
			• exposure to citizenship focus of classroom
			• low-key way to explore child's values
			• opportunity to communicate personal values
			• more information for ongoing guidance of child

Classroom Community	• see parents as valued contributors to classroom
	• build interpersonal understanding
	   - of individuals
	   - of diverse families/situations
	• build shared learning orientation
		• more understanding and empathy
		   - for individual students
		   - for parents' hopes and concerns
		   - for diverse circumstances of students
		• more comfort inviting parents into community
		• reinforce shared learning orientation
			• more knowledge of child's classroom
			• more comfort with child's classroom
			• more comfort with child's teacher
			• opportunity to contribute to the life of the classroom
			• low-risk forum for communicating with teacher

Perhaps as important as the activity-specific information generated by Homeside Activities are the open-ended comments to teachers that parents are encouraged to write. Sometimes the remarks let the teacher in on a child's concerns, for example, about teasing or a bully; sometimes they are simply observations, such as, "Carlos loves science this year"; and sometimes they comment on the value of the activity, as in the following:

> "Allison liked this one. It got us both thinking and she shared more of the day's activities with me."

> "Tyrone says he likes doing these activities because 'your parents can help you' and because it makes you 'think about things.' I think the time spent is very special for him because we always seem to learn something about each other."

> "It was a good way to have a conversation with my son. I am grateful to you for the idea."

Of course some parents might be unable or unwilling to do the activities, in which case it may be possible to find a grandparent, older sibling, neighbor, or staff member who can be a child's regular Homeside partner. For most parents, however, as uncertain as they may be about how to help their children in school, more involvement is welcome when it is introduced through specific activities within their experience and competence. Homeside Activities provide such a structure.

The particular strengths of Homeside Activities fall into three areas: academic and intellectual, citizenship, and classroom community. The chart on page 2 shows how children, teachers, and parents can all benefit in each of these areas.

Academic and Intellectual Benefits

Homeside Activities contribute to children's academic and intellectual growth in a variety of ways—most directly by providing a motivating context for children to make connections between home and school learning. Children practice critical thinking and communication skills in every activity.

Motivates Children. Children can be expected to have a stronger investment in school and academic work if it is an investment made by their parents as well. When children have a Homeside Activity to complete, they can, in effect, schedule a parent's attention and involvement.

Includes All Parents. Because the activities engage parents around universal experiences—of growing up, of having opinions, of having adult perspectives on things children are learning—the activities are inclusive and no parent need feel intimidated or incapable of contributing.

"It was a good way to have a conversation with my son."

Values Home Languages. For families whose home language is not English, the activities send the message that the school values communication in the home language. For Spanish-speakers this message is explicit since the activities are available in Spanish. For those with home languages other than Spanish or English, students will have gone over the activities in class and will be prepared to serve as "activity directors" at home.

Promotes Literacy and Thinking Skills. In doing these activities children practice literacy and thinking skills of talking, listening, synthesizing information to report to parents or back to the classroom, and comparing and evaluating information and points of view—skills that are core competencies for academic and life success.

Educates Parents about a "Thinking" Curriculum. Many parents were educated at a time when memorization and rote learning were the primary goals of schooling. Homeside Activities can introduce these parents to a "thinking" curriculum that asks open-ended questions and encourages problem solving and divergent thinking. Rather than limiting parents' role to one of monitoring homework completion, for example, Homeside Activities invite parents to participate in their children's learning experiences and allow them to enjoy their children's ideas and thought processes.

Makes Children's Past Experiences and Prior Knowledge More Accessible to the Teacher. Homeside Activities bring new areas of children's experience into the classroom, broadening the possible connections teachers can help children make when they are constructing new knowledge. When teachers and children have widely different background experiences, this can be especially important.

Citizenship Benefits

Many Homeside Activities involve children and parents in discussions of ethical behavior and principled choices about how to treat oneself and others. The activities provide parents and children with a comfortable way to exchange ideas about important values in their family.

Deepens Children's Ethical Commitment. When ethical concerns such as ways we treat a friend or how we identify "heroes" are raised at school and reinforced at home, children see their parents and teachers as partners for their ethical development. Children respond positively when the most important adults in their lives demonstrate congruent investment in their growth as kind and principled human beings.

Strengthens Children's Development as Decision Makers. The time children spend thinking about and discussing citizenship goals and ethical concerns helps them build complex understanding of these issues and prepares them to become autonomous, ethical decision makers. Homeside Activities provide a way for children to anticipate ethical choices and rehearse future behaviors.

Children practice critical thinking and communication skills in every activity

Enhances Parental Guidance. When parents and children can exchange ideas about citizenship goals and ethical concerns in the context of Homeside Activities, rather than in response to an immediate problem, the discussion can be less loaded for both. In such a context, children may be more likely to let parents into their sometimes mysterious world, and parents may welcome a conversational approach for transmitting their values.

Classroom Community Benefits

Homeside Activities structure a way to build children's and parents' personal connections to the classroom—to create a shared feeling of community.

Invites Parents into the Community. Homeside Activities are invitations to parents to learn more about the life of their children's classroom. They are also a way for parents to become comfortable communicating with their children's teacher.

Encourages Parents to Contribute Directly to the Life of the Classroom. Information that parents contribute to the classroom through Homeside Activities deepens students' understanding of each other, provides teachers with insights into children's diverse family situations, and models the school's respect for the home cultures and family experiences of all students. At the same time, Homeside Activities do not require parents who are too busy, too tired, or too embarrassed to be anyplace other than at home with their child when making their contributions.

Reinforces a Learning Orientation. A classroom community is defined by the shared goals of its members. Homeside Activities, by virtue of their content and approach, make it clear to everyone involved with the classroom that its members are learning about learning, learning about ethical behavior, and learning about how to treat one another respectfully.

How These Activities Were Developed

Homeside Activities have been piloted and field-tested in the hundreds of classrooms across the country that have participated in the Child Development Project (CDP), a comprehensive school change effort to help elementary schools become inclusive, caring communities and stimulating, supportive places to learn. Our research has identified several conditions that children need to reach their fullest social and academic potential:

- close and caring relationships with their peers and teachers;
- opportunities to practice and benefit from prosocial values;
- compelling, relevant curriculum; and
- close cooperation and communication between families and school.

A comfortable way to exchange ideas about important values

Homeside Activities are one of the many approaches CDP has developed to meet these conditions, and over the past decade that the Homeside Activities have been used in CDP schools, we have discovered many ways to make them easier for teachers to justify academically, easier for *all* parents to respond to, and "friendlier" for kids to bring home.

FIELD-TEST FEEDBACK

Feedback from teachers, parents, and students about all aspects of Homeside Activities, coupled with our own classroom and home observations, led us to strengthen and highlight many aspects of the program, especially the following:

1 Provide teachers with introductory and follow-up classroom activities that help them incorporate the Homeside Activities into their academic programs.

2 Make the academic relevance of the activities clear to parents.

3 Make no demands in the activities that might require any resources that could exclude parents from participating.

4 Streamline the amount of information provided to parents, and use simple vocabulary and syntax.

5 Make clear that the activities are voluntary and should be enjoyable.

6 Make clear that the activities are open-ended and not "tests" of children's academic performance or ability.

7 Emphasize the importance of not grading the activities or penalizing students who are unable to return them.

8 Allow at least a week for completion of the activities.

9 Represent diverse cultures in the activity poems, quotes, songs, and other references.

10 Screen all activities for cultural sensitivity.

Guidelines for Teachers

All Homeside Activities are built around parent-child conversations and usually involve students in a short drawing or writing activity. The activities for grades K–3 are addressed to adults, and adults direct the conversation; the activities for grades 4–5 are addressed to students and are student-directed. To increase both parents' and children's comfort and success in using the activities, consider the following guidelines.

Introduce the Activities Early in the Year. During back-to-school night or a similar beginning-of-the-year occasion, personally and enthusiastically inform parents about the purpose and benefits of Homeside Activities—this definitely enhances parents' responsiveness when their children begin bringing home these assignments. If you use the first Homeside Activity in your grade-level set, "Introducing Homeside Activities," it also explains the nature of these assignments. In addition to or instead of "Introducing Homeside Activities," you might send a letter to your students' parents to explain your goals for the activities (see, for example, "A Note about Homeside Activities" on page 9). And as new children enroll in your class, be sure to communicate with their parents about your Homeside Activities program.

Explain What the Activities Are and What They Are Not. Most parents appreciate these activities and enjoy the time spent with their children, but you may also meet with some resistance from parents who misunderstand them. To preclude some possible objections, it is important to present the activities in such a way that they don't appear to be a prescription for "fixing" families or for teaching parents how to communicate with their children. Be prepared to speak with parents who expect traditional homework assignments: some may need to understand that this is "real" homework, because conversation is as important to their child's development as are other assignments. Above all, emphasize that these are supposed to be enjoyable, not a burden to either the parents or the children.

Encourage Parents to Use Their Home Language. Be sure parents understand that it's perfectly fine for them to do these activities in their home language. Point out the value to their children of developing facility in their home language as well as in English.

Use Homeside Activities Often. To see that these assignments are viewed neither as a burden nor a novelty, use them frequently enough for parents and students to see them as an integral part of the classroom program (ideally, one or two times per month). When scheduling their use, keep in mind two considerations: allow families one full week to complete each activity, preferably including a weekend; also coordinate with other teachers so that a family isn't inundated by having all their children bring these activities home at the same time.

Adjust Your Own Homework Habits. Make it clear to students (as well as their parents) that these Homeside Activities do not increase their homework load, but are part of it. This may mean that you have to adjust your own homework plans so that these activities are assigned instead of, rather than in addition to, a typical assignment.

Help Students Engage Family Members. Treat Homeside Activities with the same seriousness you use for other homework, but do not penalize students when circumstances beyond their control make it impossible or counterproductive to complete an activity. If possible, help students find ways around obstacles they may encounter; when a parent is not available, for example,

Homeside Activities link children's school and home lives

encourage students to enlist the participation of other older family members or other older people. You might also have students brainstorm ways to encourage their family's participation, such as thinking ahead to when might be the best time to introduce an activity—not, for example, the night before the assignment is due, or as parents are rushing to get to work or to get dinner on the table.

Review or Rehearse the Activities in Class. All the activities are accompanied by ideas for introducing them in class and reviewing what it is that students will be doing at home. Students will feel more confident doing Homeside Activities when they have had a chance to practice or review them first. For example, when the activity asks students to interview their parents, you might have them first ask you or a partner the interview questions. In this way, students will already have an idea of what to say when they begin their dialogue with their parents; also, if their parents are not proficient in English, then the children will "know" how the assignment is supposed to go and can help their parents carry it out. Also, many teachers report that previewing the activity "jump-starts" students' enthusiasm for doing it at home.

Have Fun! Again, in considering these guidelines and planning a program of Homeside Activities, remember that flexibility and fun are key to making them work. No one needs to look for the "right" answers to questions, for the "right" conversation to take place, for the "right" products to be returned to class. Instead, the purpose and benefits of Homeside Activities are broader and perhaps more ambitious: to encourage family interactions that link children's school and home lives. We hope you will enjoy these rewarding connections among school, home, students, parents, and teachers.

Dear Family Members and Family Friends,

Welcome to Homeside Activities! Your child will bring these home to do with you once or twice a month—to add a "homeside" to the "schoolside" learning we are doing in class. These 15- to 20-minute activities

- are built around conversations between you and your child,
- deal with topics and ideas related to your child's schoolwork;
- may involve your child in a short writing or drawing activity, and
- help create a partnership between school and home.

You will find that in Homeside Activities there are no "right" or "wrong" answers, no right or wrong ways to do the activities. You can take the conversation in any direction you want, and you can have as many family members participate as you'd like. Just having these conversations is what counts, because they help your child develop thinking and language skills for life. These assignments contribute to your child's academic and social learning because

- they help you stay in touch with your child's learning;
- working with you increases your child's interest in the work;
- your child gets to practice communication skills and think about important ideas; and
- your child learns from you and sees how school learning relates to "real life."

These don't take long to do, and I'll try to give you plenty of time to fit them into your schedule. Also, teachers will plan together when to use these activities. That way, if you have several children at school, they won't all bring these home at the same time.

Thanks for taking the time to share these wonderful learning experiences with us. I hope you and your child enjoy Homeside Activities.

Your child's teacher,

UNA NOTA BREVE SOBRE
LAS ACTIVIDADES FAMILIARES

Estimados padres, familiares y amigos:

¡Bienvenidos a las Actividades Familiares! Su hija o su hijo traerá estas actividades a casa una o dos veces al mes, para realizarlas junto con Uds. Esto le añadirá una dimensión hogareña a nuestro aprendizaje escolar. Cada actividad requiere de 15 a 20 minutos. En su conjunto, las actividades

- reconocen la importancia fundamental del diálogo familiar;
- tratan ideas y temas relacionados al trabajo escolar de su hija o de su hijo;
- con frecuencia incluyen una breve actividad de dibujo o de escritura y
- ayudan a crear una mejor colaboración entre la escuela y el hogar.

Encontrará que no hay respuestas "correctas" ni "incorrectas" a las Actividades Familiares, ni tampoco maneras correctas o incorrectas de llevarlas a cabo. Puede orientar el diálogo en la dirección que guste, y solicitar la participación de todos los miembros de la familia que desee. Lo importante es el simple hecho de tener estas conversaciones en el idioma que Ud. domina, ya que ésa es la mejor manera de guiar a su hija o a su hijo y de ayudarle a desarrollar su capacidad de razonar. Si su hija o su hijo aprende a comunicarse bien en el idioma del hogar, esto le ayudará a dominar con mayor facilidad el idioma de la escuela. Y el hablar bien dos idiomas le será una gran ventaja a lo largo de su vida.

Estas tareas familiares apoyan el aprendizaje académico y social , ya que:

- le ayudan a Ud. a estar al tanto de lo que su hija o su hijo está aprendiendo en la escuela;
- el trabajar con Ud. despierta el interés de su hija o de su hijo por los trabajos escolares;
- su hija o su hijo puede ejercer sus habilidades de comunicación y pensar acerca de ideas significativas;
- su hija o su hijo aprende de Ud., y puede darse cuenta de cómo lo que aprende en la escuela se relaciona con la vida cotidiana.

Las actividades no le llevarán demasiado tiempo, y trataré de darles un buen plazo en el cual las podrán cumplir. Las maestras también coordinarán el uso de las actividades entre sí, para evitar que, si usted tiene varios niños en la misma escuela, todos le traigan actividades a casa a la misma vez.

Le agradezco el que se tome el trabajo de compartir estos valiosos momentos de aprendizaje con nosotros. Espero que disfruten las Actividades Familiares.

Atentamente,

Introducing Homeside Activities

Before Sending Home the Activity

Introduce students to Homeside Activities and have a class discussion about how these activities are different from other homework assignments. Ask students to talk with a partner about what they think they will enjoy about doing Homeside Activities with a parent or adult friend, and what might be hard about doing Homeside Activities.

Have students design covers for Homeside Activity folders on manila folders or envelopes. Send the folders home with the first Homeside Activity. Have students keep completed Homeside Activities in their folders, until they bring the folders and completed activities home again with the final Homeside Activity of the year.

Follow-Up

Have students share their reactions to the first Homeside Activity. What did they enjoy about the activity? What did their parent or adult friend enjoy? What problems did students encounter? What was most interesting about the activity? Most surprising? Give students a chance to show and explain their pictures to their partners or to the class.

Introducing Homeside Activities

Dear Student,

You are in charge of this Homeside Activity, which means you are in charge of finding an adult to do it with you, finding time you both have free to do it, explaining and "directing" the activity, making sure the adult signs it, and bringing it back to class. Please find about 20 minutes that you can spend on the activity with a parent or other adult—a neighbor, grandparent, older brother or sister, or family friend. If you'd like, get a bunch of people involved!

One of the most important reasons for doing this activity is that you and the adult will learn things from each other about what you think, feel, know, and want to know. In class we can then also learn from each other, when we share what we have learned at home. Just be sure to ask the adults for permission to pass along what they say—and don't forget to thank them for contributing to our class's learning!

Tell a parent or other adult that you will be bringing home some Homeside Activities this year.

Explain that these activities ask you to talk with a parent or other adult about topics connected to your class work. Show the adult the folder you made for your Homeside Activities, and explain your design.

Talk with the adult about how the Homeside Activities will be different from other homework. Then tell each other what you might like about having these "homework" conversations.

Take notes on the back of this page.

NOTES

Ways the Homeside Activities will be different from other homework:

....

....

....

....

Some things the adult might like about your "homework" conversations:

....

....

....

....

Some things you might like about your "homework" conversations:

....

....

....

....

Comments

After you have completed this activity, each of you please sign your name and the date below. If you have any comments, please write them in the space provided.

Signatures   **Date**

Please return this activity to school. Thank you.

This School Year

Before Sending Home the Activity

Send this activity home after you have held a start-the-year class meeting or have reviewed with your class what this new school year will entail.

Before sending the activity home, ask the class for suggestions about making this Homeside Activity successful.

Follow-Up

Have students do partner interviews about their goals and challenges for this school year.

This School Year

Dear Student,

You are in charge of this Homeside Activity, which means you are in charge of finding an adult to do it with you, finding time you both have free to do it, explaining and "directing" the activity, making sure the adult signs it, and bringing it back to class. Please find about 20 minutes that you can spend on the activity with a parent or other adult—a neighbor, grandparent, older brother or sister, or family friend. If you'd like, get a bunch of people involved!

One of the most important reasons for doing this activity is that you and the adult will learn things from each other about what you think, feel, know, and want to know. In class we can then also learn from each other, when we share what we have learned at home. Just be sure to ask the adults for permission to pass along what they say—and don't forget to thank them for contributing to our class's learning!

Tell a parent or another adult what you think this new school year will be like. What do you look forward to? What don't you look forward to?

Name three things that you would like to learn or get better at this year. Describe why these might be easy or hard to do.

Then ask your parent or the adult if there is any subject he or she would like to have learned better in elementary school. Take notes on the back of this page.

NOTES

What I look forward to this school year:

....

....

What I don't look forward to this school year:

....

....

Three things I would like to learn or get better at this year:

1 ....

....

2 ....

....

3 ....

....

Something the adult wishes he or she had learned better in elementary school:

....

....

Comments

After you have completed
this activity, each of you
please sign your name and
the date below. If you have
any comments, please
write them in the space
provided.

....

....

....

....

Signatures   **Date**

_____   _____   _____

Please return this activity to school. Thank you.

Everyday Math

Before Sending Home the Activity

This is a good activity to do early in the school year, to reinforce students' sense of math being "real" and relevant to their lives. Before sending home the activity, ask students for examples of how they think their parents, or any adults, use math in daily life. Also ask the class for suggestions for making this Homeside Activity successful.

Follow-Up

Have students make lists of how they think adults use math in everyday life (including any results they got from their home interviews); then have partners create Venn diagrams showing the elements common to both of their lists and those that are unique to each list. Or, depending on what specific mathematical topic your class is studying, you could create a class math exercise using students' interview results (e.g., percentage of adults who said they use math to balance a checkbook, to alter a recipe, and so on).

Everyday Math

Dear Student,

You are in charge of this Homeside Activity, which means you are in charge of finding an adult to do it with you, finding time you both have free to do it, explaining and "directing" the activity, making sure the adult signs it, and bringing it back to class. Please find about 20 minutes that you can spend on the activity with a parent or other adult—a neighbor, grandparent, older brother or sister, or family friend. If you'd like, get a bunch of people involved!

One of the most important reasons for doing this activity is that you and the adult will learn things from each other about what you think, feel, know, and want to know. In class we can then also learn from each other, when we share what we have learned at home. Just be sure to ask the adults for permission to pass along what they say—and don't forget to thank them for contributing to our class's learning!

Use the questions on the back of this page to interview a parent or another adult about how he or she uses mathematics in everyday life. Also find out about how the adult learned math when he or she was in school. You can make up your own interview questions, too. Take notes in the space provided.

INTERVIEW QUESTIONS

Can you think of two or three ways you commonly use math?

....

....

....

....

Do you have any quick tricks or mathematical "short cuts" that you use? If so, can you explain them to me?

....

....

....

....

Tell me a story about learning or doing math in school when you were a child.

....

....

....

....

....

....

Comments

After you have completed this activity, each of you please sign your name and the date below. If you have any comments, please write them in the space provided.

Signatures   Date

_____   _____   _____

Please return this activity to school. Thank you.

Poetry Performance

Before Sending Home the Activity

This activity will be more successful if students are familiar with poetry and comfortable reading it. If you have not yet used poetry in your classroom, begin introducing a variety of poems in the weeks before you have students do this activity.

A week before sending home the activity, have students select a poem to read to a parent or adult friend. Have a wide range of poetry available—from humorous poems by Shel Silverstein and David McCord to serious poetry that describes a scene, event, or cause for reflection. Make sure you have poems available in other languages if you have students whose home language is not English. (If you have Spanish-speakers, you may want to include some humorous poems by Maria Elena Walsh, in addition to more serious poetry.)

Have students practice reciting their poems to a partner. Encourage students to experiment with a variety of reciting styles before deciding on the most effective one. Some students may enjoy learning their poems by heart. Others will prefer the support of reading from printed text. Either way, the success of the recital will depend on how familiar and comfortable the student is with the poem he or she has chosen.

Go over the Homeside Activity directions and have students copy their poem on the back of the page.

Follow-Up

Discuss how the activity went for students. How was it successful? How was it not successful? Why? What might students do differently next time? What would they do the same way? How did students feel during the recital? What did the adult appreciate about the recital? What were some similarities and differences between what students and adults liked about the poems? Organize frequent opportunities for students to recite poetry—to classmates, buddies, other classes, and parents. Invite a poet to your class, or attend a poetry recital in your community.

Poetry Performance

Dear Student,

You are in charge of this Homeside Activity, which means you are in charge of finding an adult to do it with you, finding time you both have free to do it, explaining and "directing" the activity, making sure the adult signs it, and bringing it back to class. Please find about 20 minutes that you can spend on the activity with a parent or other adult—a neighbor, grandparent, older brother or sister, or family friend. If you'd like, get a bunch of people involved!

One of the most important reasons for doing this activity is that you and the adult will learn things from each other about what you think, feel, know, and want to know. In class we can then also learn from each other, when we share what we have learned at home. Just be sure to ask the adults for permission to pass along what they say—and don't forget to thank them for contributing to our class's learning!

Recite or perform the poem you have chosen for a parent or adult friend.

Tell the adult why you chose the poem. Underline two or three of your favorite lines or phrases and explain what you like about them.

Then ask the adult to underline two or three favorite lines or phrases. Compare and discuss your choices. Take notes on the back of this page.

NOTES

My favorite part of the poem, and why:

....

....

....

....

....

....

The adult's favorite part of the poem, and why:

....

....

....

....

....

....

Comments

....

After you have completed this activity, each of you please sign your name and the date below. If you have any comments, please write them in the space provided.

....

....

....

....

Signatures   **Date**

_____   _____   _____

Please return this activity to school. Thank you.

My Opinion

Before Sending Home the Activity

Have each student choose a current issue or event, related to something the class is studying, about which he or she feels strongly. The issue may be of local, state, national, or international interest. Explain that you want students to express their opinion in writing to an audience such as elected officials, bureaucrats, or newspapers. Ask students to think about what the most appropriate audience might be and how they might express their opinion most convincingly.

To help students support their opinions with information about their chosen issues, make available a variety of publications and video clips as resources. Encourage students to clarify their ideas before writing by discussing their issue with classmates who share an interest in the same topic.

Before sending the activity home, help students think about the importance of respecting different opinions and disagreeing respectfully. Ask the class for suggestions about how to make this Homeside Activity successful.

Follow-Up

Have students describe doing the activity at home. How did they handle differences of opinion? In which areas did they agree and disagree with the adult? Did students' or adults' opinions change as a result of talking with one another? Were there any surprises?

Have students send their letters, and encourage them to share with the class any replies they receive. Have students follow their issues and report to the class any news related to them.

My Opinion

Dear Student,

You are in charge of this Homeside Activity, which means you are in charge of finding an adult to do it with you, finding time you both have free to do it, explaining and "directing" the activity, making sure the adult signs it, and bringing it back to class. Please find about 20 minutes that you can spend on the activity with a parent or other adult—a neighbor, grandparent, older brother or sister, or family friend. If you'd like, get a bunch of people involved!

One of the most important reasons for doing this activity is that you and the adult will learn things from each other about what you think, feel, know, and want to know. In class we can then also learn from each other, when we share what we have learned at home. Just be sure to ask the adults for permission to pass along what they say—and don't forget to thank them for contributing to our class's learning!

Describe to a parent or adult friend the current issue you are concerned about. Explain why it is important to you and why you wrote to the person or publication you did.

Then read your letter to the adult. Ask for the adult's opinions about the issue.

Discuss ways your opinions are similar and ways they are different. Take notes on your discussion on the back of this page.

N O T E S

Ways Our Ideas Are Similar

Ways Our Ideas Are Different

Comments

After you have completed this activity, each of you please sign your name and the date below. If you have any comments, please write them in the space provided.

Signatures

Date

Please return this activity to school. Thank you.

Then and Now

Before Sending Home the Activity

This activity can be used in conjunction with various social studies, current events, poetry, or music classes. Read the poem aloud to the class (you might want to read it aloud by yourself a couple of times to practice the musical cadence of the "clackety clacks"). Ask if any students are familiar with the music and dance described in the poem, and if they know anyone who grew up when those were popular. Also be prepared to explain the "bones" referred to in the poem, based on this note by its author:

> "'Grandma's Bones' tells about some of the activities people enjoyed when I was a teenager in the nineteen-forties. Some of the boys I knew played the instrument called 'bones,' . . . moving their shoulders and heads to the rhythm as they played. Our ancestors had played this instrument in Africa, often using the bones of animals."

Go over the activity with the class, and encourage students to add interview questions about any other pop culture topics they are interested in.

Before sending the activity home, ask the class for suggestions about making this Homeside Activity successful.

Follow-Up

Have students use their notes to write a comparison of the adult's musical taste and their own tastes at the same age, including why they think these might be different (or you may want to create a different writing assignment, tailored to how you relate this to other curriculum).

Grandma's Bones

Grandma grew up
in the nineteen-forties
she can still do the jitterbug
a dance they used to do
to the music of Duke Ellington,
Benny Carter, Count Basie
and such

she can spin a yo-yo
much better than I
and sometimes she puts two sticks called bones
between the knuckles
of one hand and goes

clack clack clackety
clackety clack
clackety clackety clackety
clack clack
uh clackety clack
uh clackety clack
clack clack clackety
clackety clack!

—Eloise Greenfield*

Then and Now

Dear Student,

You are in charge of this Homeside Activity, which means you are in charge of finding an adult to do it with you, finding time you both have free to do it, explaining and "directing" the activity, making sure the adult signs it, and bringing it back to class. Please find about 20 minutes that you can spend on the activity with a parent or other adult—a neighbor, grandparent, older brother or sister, or family friend. If you'd like, get a bunch of people involved!

One of the most important reasons for doing this activity is that you and the adult will learn things from each other about what you think, feel, know, and want to know. In class we can then also learn from each other, when we share what we have learned at home. Just be sure to ask the adults for permission to pass along what they say—and don't forget to thank them for contributing to our class's learning!

With a parent or other adult, read the attached poem, "Grandma's Bones." Use the questions on the back of this page to interview the adult about the music, dances, and styles that were popular when he or she was your age.

Add your own interview questions if you'd like, and take notes in the space provided. In class we will use these notes for a writing exercise.

INTERVIEW QUESTIONS

When you were my age, what were your favorite singing groups? Why?

....

....

....

What dances did you do?

....

....

....

What kinds of clothes and hairstyles were popular then?

....

....

....

What else do you particularly remember was popular in those days?

....

....

....

....

Comments

After you have completed
this activity, each of you
please sign your name and
the date below. If you have
any comments, please
write them in the space
provided.

....

....

....

....

Signatures   **Date**

_____   _____   _____

Please return this activity to school. Thank you.

Personal Time Capsule

Before Sending Home the Activity

Have a class discussion about time capsules—their purpose, what items they might contain, and so forth. Discuss the time capsule in terms of the area of history you are studying in class: What artifacts help us understand what life was like in that civilization during that time in history? What do we learn about the people of that time? Describe the Homeside Activity, explaining that while most time capsules contain items that tell about a particular civilization, you want students to think of time capsules that tell about particular people—themselves. Ask students to make suggestions about things that might be included in their personal time capsules. To avoid disappointment, make sure students understand that the assignment is an exercise of the imagination (and communication) and that they will not be creating and storing real time capsules.

Before sending the activity home, ask the class for suggestions about making this Homeside Activity successful.

Follow-Up

Give students a chance to talk about doing the activity at home, and invite volunteers to describe the contents of their time capsules (including the things the adults added). Students could also share their lists with a partner, or students who would like to participate could play a game where they try to match anonymous lists with the classmates who generated them.

Extend the activity by having students create a classroom time capsule that could be stored at school for children of the future.

Personal Time Capsule

Dear Student,

You are in charge of this Homeside Activity, which means you are in charge of finding an adult to do it with you, finding time you both have free to do it, explaining and "directing" the activity, making sure the adult signs it, and bringing it back to class. Please find about 20 minutes that you can spend on the activity with a parent or other adult—a neighbor, grandparent, older brother or sister, or family friend. If you'd like, get a bunch of people involved!

One of the most important reasons for doing this activity is that you and the adult will learn things from each other about what you think, feel, know, and want to know. In class we can then also learn from each other, when we share what we have learned at home. Just be sure to ask the adults for permission to pass along what they say—and don't forget to thank them for contributing to our class's learning!

On the back of this page, list five to ten items that you would include in a personal time capsule to be opened in twenty-five years— things that tell something about who you are and what you like.

Tell a parent or adult friend about the things you chose and why you would include them in your time capsule. What does each item say about you?

Ask the adult to think of any other items he or she would add to complete the picture of who you are. Write those on the back of this page.

MY PERSONAL TIME CAPSULE

Items I Chose for My Time Capsule

Other Items Added by the Adult

_____

_____

_____

_____

_____

_____

_____

_____

_____

_____

_____

Comments

After you have completed this activity, each of you please sign your name and the date below. If you have any comments, please write them in the space provided.

Signatures

Date

Please return this activity to school. Thank you.

Walking Tall

Before Sending Home the Activity

Read the poem aloud to the class. Talk with students about why the poem is called "January," and talk about different cultures' celebrations of the new year (many of which don't occur in January). Ask them to think about what makes this an appropriate poem for a new year (or a new semester)—what feelings and attitudes characterize the new year?

Before sending the activity home, ask the class for suggestions about making this Homeside Activity successful.

Follow-Up

Have a whole-class discussion about what students think it means to "walk tall." Then have students think of reasons that the class has for walking tall. This is also a good opportunity to reaffirm the class norms agreed upon in the first semester and renew students' sense of the classroom community they have been building.

Walking Tall

Dear Student,

You are in charge of this Homeside Activity, which means you are in charge of finding an adult to do it with you, finding time you both have free to do it, explaining and "directing" the activity, making sure the adult signs it, and bringing it back to class. Please find about 20 minutes that you can spend on the activity with a parent or other adult—a neighbor, grandparent, older brother or sister, or family friend. If you'd like, get a bunch of people involved!

One of the most important reasons for doing this activity is that you and the adult will learn things from each other about what you think, feel, know, and want to know. In class we can then also learn from each other, when we share what we have learned at home. Just be sure to ask the adults for permission to pass along what they say—and don't forget to thank them for contributing to our class's learning!

Read the following poem, "January," with a parent or other adult. Talk about what you each think it means to "walk tall in the world." Why do you think the mother gives this advice at the beginning of a new year?

On the back of this page, make a list of reasons you each have for walking tall. Take turns suggesting reasons for each other's list, and only include reasons you both agree on.

January

"Walk tall in the world,"
says Mama
to Everett Anderson.
"The year is new
and so are the days,
walk tall in the world,"
she says.

—Lucille Clifton*

* From *Everett Anderson's Year* by Lucille Clifton. Copyright © 1978 by Lucille Clifton. Reprinted by permission of Henry Holt & Co., Inc.

WALKING TALL

My Reasons for Walking Tall

Adult's Reasons for Walking Tall

Comments

After you have completed this activity, each of you please sign your name and the date below. If you have any comments, please write them in the space provided.

Signatures

Date

Please return this activity to school. Thank you.

Family Folklore

Before Sending Home the Activity

This activity is designed to accompany material on family or cultural folklore—stories, rituals, and traditions that help define our histories, values, and identities within and across generations.

If any of your students have a hard time finding family members to do these Homeside Activities with them, or if they have broad definitions of the word "family," encourage them to turn to adults other than immediate family members.

Before sending the activity home, ask the class for suggestions about making this Homeside Activity successful.

Follow-Up

Have students do partner interviews to find out about each other's family folklore. Give students a chance to tell their partners' stories to the whole class. (Emphasize that they need to check with their partners first, to make sure it's okay to tell their stories.)

Family Folklore

Dear Student,

You are in charge of this Homeside Activity, which means you are in charge of finding an adult to do it with you, finding time you both have free to do it, explaining and "directing" the activity, making sure the adult signs it, and bringing it back to class. Please find about 20 minutes that you can spend on the activity with a parent or other adult—a neighbor, grandparent, older brother or sister, or family friend. If you'd like, get a bunch of people involved!

One of the most important reasons for doing this activity is that you and the adult will learn things from each other about what you think, feel, know, and want to know. In class we can then also learn from each other, when we share what we have learned at home. Just be sure to ask the adults for permission to pass along what they say—and don't forget to thank them for contributing to our class's learning!

Interview a parent or other family member about your family history. Ask the questions below. (The person you interview may not have stories to tell about all of these questions.) Then on the back of this page write a summary of one of the stories to share in class.

INTERVIEW QUESTIONS

- Is there a family hero or "character" that you could tell me about?

- Do you have a story about how a family joke or saying got started?

- Can you tell me a story about a family courtship or wedding?

- What is your favorite story about when you were growing up?

FAMILY FOLKLORE STORY

In the space below, write a summary of one of the stories from the interview.

_____

_____

_____

_____

_____

_____

_____

_____

_____

_____

_____

_____

Comments

After you have completed
this activity, each of you
please sign your name and
the date below. If you have
any comments, please
write them in the space
provided.

_____

_____

_____

_____

Signatures   ### Date

_____ _____   _____

Please return this activity to school. Thank you.

Harvey

Before Sending Home the Activity

Have a class discussion about friendship—what it means to be a good friend and what it means to have a good friend. Ask students to generate a list of qualities or behaviors that they would want in a good friend. (You may get some additional ideas if you then ask them to generate a list of qualities or behaviors that would be undesirable in a friend.) Ask if they think their ideas about what makes a good friend have changed as they have grown older. What is important to them now that wasn't so important when they were five or six?

Before sending the activity home, ask the class for suggestions about making this Home Activity successful.

Follow-up

You may wish to save the lists of qualities and behaviors from the class discussion; then, after the students have done the activity at home, you can have them compare the class's ideas with the qualities and behaviors of friends that the adults share with students in the home discussions.

Harvey

Harvey doesn't laugh about how I stay short while everybody grows.

Harvey remembers I like jellybeans—except black.

Harvey lends me shirts I don't have to give back.

I'm scared of ghosts and only Harvey knows.

Harvey thinks I will when I say someday I will marry Margie Rose.

Harvey shares his lemonade—sip for sip.

He whispers "zip" when I forget to zip.

He swears I don't have funny-looking toes.

Harvey calls me up when I'm in bed with a sore throat and runny nose.

Harvey says I'm nice—but not *too* nice.

And if there is a train to Paradise,

I won't get on it unless Harvey goes.

                    —Judith Viorst*

* From *If I Were in Charge of the World and other worries,* published by Atheneum Publishers, an imprint of Macmillan Publishing Company. Copyright © 1981 by Judith Viorst.

Harvey

Dear Student,

You are in charge of this Homeside Activity, which means you are in charge of finding an adult to do it with you, finding time you both have free to do it, explaining and "directing" the activity, making sure the adult signs it, and bringing it back to class. Please find about 20 minutes that you can spend on the activity with a parent or other adult—a neighbor, grandparent, older brother or sister, or family friend. If you'd like, get a bunch of people involved!

One of the most important reasons for doing this activity is that you and the adult will learn things from each other about what you think, feel, know, and want to know. In class we can then also learn from each other, when we share what we have learned at home. Just be sure to ask the adults for permission to pass along what they say—and don't forget to thank them for contributing to our class's learning!

The attached poem, "Harvey," is one person's description of a special friend. Read the poem with a parent or adult friend, and share your ideas about what makes Harvey a good friend.

Then use the questions on the back of this page to interview each other about friendships. Take notes about your conversation in the space provided.

HOMESIDE ACTIVITY

INTERVIEW QUESTIONS

What qualities does Harvey have that you think you would like in a friend?

Student:

Adult:

....

....

....

What qualities are most important to you in a close friend?

Student:

Adult:

....

....

....

(For the adult only) Do you remember a best friend from elementary school? Why do you remember this person?

....

....

....

Who is a close friend now? Why is this person important to you? Why do you think you are important to this friend?

Student:

Adult:

....

....

....

Comments

After you have completed this activity, each of you please sign your name and the date below. If you have any comments, please write them in the space provided.

....

....

....

....

....

Signatures

Date

Please return this activity to school. Thank you.

HARVEY

Trading Places

Before Sending Home the Activity

Tell the class about the Homeside Activity, and share your own fantasy about trading places with another person. (If possible, think of a character from a book the class is familiar with.) Invite students to tell the whole class or a partner about a character with whom they would like to trade places for a day, and why.

Before sending the activity home, ask the class for suggestions about making this Homeside Activity successful.

Follow-Up

Have students share with a partner what they wrote on the activity sheet.

Students may enjoy writing stories (or cartoons) about trading places with the character of their choice. (Assuming another identity—either deliberately or by mistake—is a common theme in literature. Students may enjoy hearing such a tale, for example, Sid Fleischman's *The Whipping Boy,* which is the story of a prince and his whipping boy who exchange places.)

Trading Places

Dear Student,

You are in charge of this Homeside Activity, which means you are in charge of finding an adult to do it with you, finding time you both have free to do it, explaining and "directing" the activity, making sure the adult signs it, and bringing it back to class. Please find about 20 minutes that you can spend on the activity with a parent or other adult—a neighbor, grandparent, older brother or sister, or family friend. If you'd like, get a bunch of people involved!

One of the most important reasons for doing this activity is that you and the adult will learn things from each other about what you think, feel, know, and want to know. In class we can then also learn from each other, when we share what we have learned at home. Just be sure to ask the adults for permission to pass along what they say—and don't forget to thank them for contributing to our class's learning!

When we read stories and novels in class, we often talk about what life might look like from a particular character's point of view.

For this Homeside Activity, tell a family member or family friend about one of these characters with whom you would like to trade places for one day. Why would you like to be this person? How might the character feel about being you for a day?

Then give the adult a chance to talk about a character (or real person) with whom he or she would like to trade places for a day. Take notes about your discussion on the back of this page.

NOTES

The character I would trade places with:

Student:

....

....

....

Adult:

....

....

....

Why I would like to trade places with this character:

Student:

....

....

....

....

Adult:

....

....

....

....

How this character might feel about being me for a day:

Student:

....

....

....

....

Adult:

....

....

....

....

Comments

After you have completed this activity, each of you please sign your name and the date below. If you have any comments, please write them in the space provided.

....

....

....

....

....

Signatures **Date**

_____   _____   _____

Please return this activity to school. Thank you.

They Cut Down Three Trees

Before Sending Home the Activity

In connection with a study about environmental issues, read aloud the poem "They Cut Down Three Trees" to the class. Have partners or small groups read the poem aloud together and discuss what they like or don't like about it. Then have partners or small groups discuss how a newspaper or television reporter would have described the same event. (Alternative: how a dramatist or choreographer might have staged it without words.) Finally, have the class discuss the following question:

- How do you think the poet felt about watching those three trees being cut down?

Before sending the activity home, ask the class for suggestions about making this Homeside Activity successful.

Follow-Up

Have students talk about the adults' feelings about the cutting down of trees and the reasons for these feelings. Then have the class discuss how adults' and children's feelings about the cutting down of trees are alike and different.

They Cut Down Three Trees

Dear Student,

You are in charge of this Homeside Activity, which means you are in charge of finding an adult to do it with you, finding time you both have free to do it, explaining and "directing" the activity, making sure the adult signs it, and bringing it back to class. Please find about 20 minutes that you can spend on the activity with a parent or other adult—a neighbor, grandparent, older brother or sister, or family friend. If you'd like, get a bunch of people involved!

One of the most important reasons for doing this activity is that you and the adult will learn things from each other about what you think, feel, know, and want to know. In class we can then also learn from each other, when we share what we have learned at home. Just be sure to ask the adults for permission to pass along what they say—and don't forget to thank them for contributing to our class's learning!

Tell your parent or adult friend something about the environmental concerns your class has been studying. Then read the poem below to that person.

Talk about what feelings you think the poem communicates about the three trees being cut down. Then discuss with the adult how you each feel about trees being cut down. List these feelings on the back of this page.

They Cut Down Three Trees

—To Ernesto Halffter

There were three.
(The day came with its axes.)
There were two.
(Skimming wings of plated silver.)
There was one.
There were none.
(It left the water naked.)

—Federico García Lorca*

* From *The Cricket Sings* by Federico García Lorca, © 1980 published by New Directions.

NOTES

Adult's Feelings about Trees Being Cut Down

My Feelings about Trees Being Cut Down

....

....

....

....

....

....

....

....

....

....

....

....

....

....

....

....

....

....

....

....

....

....

....

....

....

....

Comments
....

After you have completed
this activity, each of you
please sign your name and
the date below. If you have
any comments, please
write them in the space
provided.

....

....

....

....

Signatures   **Date**

_____   _____   _____

Please return this activity to school. Thank you.

Spring

Before Sending Home the Activity

Natural phenomena are frequently represented in human form; examples of this can be found in myths, stories, and art, as well as our practice of giving hurricanes human names. Introduce some examples of the personification of natural phenomena (for example, read a myth such as the story of Persephone or show a painting such as Botticelli's "Birth of Venus"). Then ask students, "If spring were a person, what would he or she be like?" Have a brief discussion. Ask, for example, "Would spring be male or female? Young or old? What kind of clothing would spring wear? What other accessories might he or she wear?" and so on. Have students draw pictures of spring in a human form. Then have them make notes on their Homeside Activity sheet about the symbolism in their pictures; for the activity, they will explain their pictures to an adult at home.

Before sending the activity home, ask the class for suggestions about making this Homeside Activity successful.

Follow-Up

Have the class categorize students' and adults' feelings and plans for spring. Talk about how some of these ideas are expressed in students' drawings.

Spring

Dear Student,

You are in charge of this Homeside Activity, which means you are in charge of finding an adult to do it with you, finding time you both have free to do it, explaining and "directing" the activity, making sure the adult signs it, and bringing it back to class. Please find about 20 minutes that you can spend on the activity with a parent or other adult—a neighbor, grandparent, older brother or sister, or family friend. If you'd like, get a bunch of people involved!

One of the most important reasons for doing this activity is that you and the adult will learn things from each other about what you think, feel, know, and want to know. In class we can then also learn from each other, when we share what we have learned at home. Just be sure to ask the adults for permission to pass along what they say—and don't forget to thank them for contributing to our class's learning!

Tell a parent or other adult about your picture of spring. Describe what you enjoy about spring and what you look forward to doing. Use the notes you recorded on the back of this sheet to help you explain your ideas.

Ask your parent or other adult to tell you what he or she enjoys about spring and what he or she looks forward to doing. Take notes about the adult's response in the space provided on the back of this page.

HOMESIDE ACTIVITY

NOTES

What my picture of spring symbolizes:

What I enjoy about spring, and why:

What I look forward to doing in spring, and why:

What an adult enjoys about spring, and why:

What an adult looks forward to doing in spring, and why:

Comments

After you have completed this activity, each of you please sign your name and the date below. If you have any comments, please write them in the space provided.

Signatures   **Date**

Please return this activity to school. Thank you.

Group Work

Before Sending Home the Activity

Make sure that students have many experiences working in cooperative groups before you use this Homeside Activity.

Have the class do a cooperative group activity the day you assign this Homeside Activity. During the wrap-up, spend time discussing what went well during group work, what didn't go well, and how problems were solved by the groups. Use the terms "benefits" and "burdens," as on the activity sheet; if necessary, help students understand what those terms mean.

Explain the Homeside Activity, and point out that students may choose any cooperative group activity to describe to the adult, not necessarily the activity just completed.

Before sending the activity home, ask the class for suggestions about making this Homeside Activity successful.

Follow-Up

Give students a chance to describe doing the activity at home. Then have students work in small groups to discuss their lists of benefits and burdens. Have groups choose one benefit and one burden and present these to the class in whatever form they choose—drama, art, writing, and so on.

(The group discussions and presentations may provide helpful clues about how group work is going in your class. For example, if "One person has to do all the work" is a dominant burden, you may want to spend more time helping students figure out ways of dividing group work more fairly.)

Group Work

Dear Student,

You are in charge of this Homeside Activity, which means you are in charge of finding an adult to do it with you, finding time you both have free to do it, explaining and "directing" the activity, making sure the adult signs it, and bringing it back to class. Please find about 20 minutes that you can spend on the activity with a parent or other adult—a neighbor, grandparent, older brother or sister, or family friend. If you'd like, get a bunch of people involved!

One of the most important reasons for doing this activity is that you and the adult will learn things from each other about what you think, feel, know, and want to know. In class we can then also learn from each other, when we share what we have learned at home. Just be sure to ask the adults for permission to pass along what they say—and don't forget to thank them for contributing to our class's learning!

Tell a parent or adult friend about a classroom small-group project. Then interview the adult about a time when the adult worked with a group of people to do a job. For example, you could each give your ideas about the following:

• what was most helpful about working with others

• what was most difficult

• what problems your group had, and how you solved them

On the back of this page, together list the "benefits" (good things) and "burdens" (not-so-good things) of working with a group of people on a project.

GROUP WORK

Benefits of Working with a Group   Burdens of Working with a Group

....

....

....

....

....

....

....

....

....

....

....

....

Comments
....

After you have completed
this activity, each of you
please sign your name and
the date below. If you have
any comments, please
write them in the space
provided.

....

....

....

....

....

Signatures   **Date**

_____   _____   _____

Please return this activity to school. Thank you.

Speech to the Young

Before Sending Home the Activity

Read the poem "Speech to the Young" aloud to the class two or three times (or have students who have practiced it in advance read it aloud). Have a class discussion about what the poem means. (Don't have students analyze the poem in detail. Rather, encourage them to form a general impression.) Have students practice reading the poem aloud to a partner in preparation for bringing it home.

Before sending the activity home, ask the class for suggestions about making this Homeside Activity successful.

Follow-Up

Give students a chance to read their speeches to the class. If students are interested, give them time to revise their speeches and compile illustrated final drafts to make a class book or newsletter.

Speech to the Young

Say to them,
say to the down-keepers,
the sun-slappers,
the self-soilers,
the harmony-hushers,
"Even if you are not ready for day
it cannot always be night."
You will be right.
For that is the hard home-run.

Live not for battles won,
Live not for the-end-of-the-song.
Live in the along.

—Gwendolyn Brooks*

N O T E S

What we think the poem means:

....
....
....
....

Advice we would give young people:

....
....
....
....

* © 1991 by Gwendolyn Brooks from *Blacks,* Third World Press, Chicago, 1991.

Speech to the Young

Dear Student,

You are in charge of this Homeside Activity, which means you are in charge of finding an adult to do it with you, finding time you both have free to do it, explaining and "directing" the activity, making sure the adult signs it, and bringing it back to class. Please find about 20 minutes that you can spend on the activity with a parent or other adult—a neighbor, grandparent, older brother or sister, or family friend. If you'd like, get a bunch of people involved!

One of the most important reasons for doing this activity is that you and the adult will learn things from each other about what you think, feel, know, and want to know. In class we can then also learn from each other, when we share what we have learned at home. Just be sure to ask the adults for permission to pass along what they say—and don't forget to thank them for contributing to our class's learning!

Read the attached poem, "Speech to the Young," with a parent or other adult.

Discuss with the adult what you think the poem means. Talk with the adult about advice you would give to young people. (The two of you may agree or disagree about what is important.) If you'd like, take brief notes on the attached page.

Use the ideas from your discussion to write your own "Speech to the Young" on the back of this page.

My Speech to the Young

_____

_____

_____

_____

_____

_____

_____

_____

_____

_____

_____

_____

_____

Comments

After you have completed
this activity, each of you
please sign your name and
the date below. If you have
any comments, please
write them in the space
provided.

_____

_____

_____

_____

_____

Signatures   **Date**

_____ _____   _____

Please return this activity to school. Thank you.

School Year Collage

Before Sending Home the Activity

Explain the activity, and have students make collages about their school year using words and images cut from magazines and newspapers. (They could also use colored pens or pencils to add to the collage.) You may want to make your own collage or show collages by artists to inspire your students. Have partners tell each other about their collages and the school year, and then provide time for students to modify or add to their collages following the partner discussions.

Have students make notes to themselves answering the questions on the Homeside Activity page. They will be able to use these notes in their conversations at home.

Before sending the activity home, ask the class for suggestions about making this Homeside Activity successful.

Follow-Up

Have students share highlights of the activity and thoughts about their academic, social, and personal learning this year. Have students display their collages so they can see each others' work.

School Year Collage

Dear Student,

You are in charge of this Homeside Activity, which means you are in charge of finding an adult to do it with you, finding time you both have free to do it, explaining and "directing" the activity, making sure the adult signs it, and bringing it back to class. Please find about 20 minutes that you can spend on the activity with a parent or other adult—a neighbor, grandparent, older brother or sister, or family friend. If you'd like, get a bunch of people involved!

One of the most important reasons for doing this activity is that you and the adult will learn things from each other about what you think, feel, know, and want to know. In class we can then also learn from each other, when we share what we have learned at home. Just be sure to ask the adults for permission to pass along what they say—and don't forget to thank them for contributing to our class's learning!

Show a parent or adult friend your collage about the school year. Talk about the words and images you included in your collage.

Use the notes you wrote on the back of this page to help you describe your collage: what it shows about your experiences, the highlights of the year, favorite projects or subjects, what your learned about yourself and others.

Then ask the adult to help you with the final item, about what the adult has learned from you.

NOTES FOR MY CONVERSATION AT HOME

Ideas about my collage:

What I learned from a special project or subject I studied:

Something I learned about people this year:

Something I learned about myself this year:

INTERVIEW QUESTION

After you discuss your notes with an adult, ask the adult to write or dictate a sentence or two describing "something the adult learned about me this year." Write it in the space below.

Comments

After you have completed this activity, each of you please sign your name and the date below. If you have any comments, please write them in the space provided.

Signatures   **Date**

Please return this activity to school. Thank you.

School Year Summary

Before Sending Home the Activity

This is a good activity to do in conjunction with an "end-the-year" activity. Before sending the activity home, ask the class for suggestions about making this Homeside Activity successful.

Follow-Up

Have partners interview each other about their memories of the school year and the memories of the adults they interviewed. Encourage them to discuss any similarities and differences between their favorite memories and the adults' favorite memories. If they're the same, why might that be? If they're different, why might that be?

School Year Summary

Dear Student,

You are in charge of this Homeside Activity, which means you are in charge of finding an adult to do it with you, finding time you both have free to do it, explaining and "directing" the activity, making sure the adult signs it, and bringing it back to class. Please find about 20 minutes that you can spend on the activity with a parent or other adult—a neighbor, grandparent, older brother or sister, or family friend. If you'd like, get a bunch of people involved!

One of the most important reasons for doing this activity is that you and the adult will learn things from each other about what you think, feel, know, and want to know. In class we can then also learn from each other, when we share what we have learned at home. Just be sure to ask the adults for permission to pass along what they say—and don't forget to thank them for contributing to our class's learning!

Discuss this past school year with a parent or other adult. Review your favorite and least favorite memories of the year.

Then find out some of the things the adult remembers about your year in school. What is the adult's favorite memory?

Take notes on the back of this page.

NOTES

My favorite memories of my school year:

....

....

....

....

My least favorite memories of my school year:

....

....

....

....

Adult's favorite memories of my school year:

....

....

....

....

....

Comments

After you have completed this activity, each of you please sign your name and the date below. If you have any comments, please write them in the space provided.

....

....

....

....

Signatures   **Date**

_____   _____   _____

Please return this activity to school. Thank you.

Homeside Activities in Review

Before Sending Home the Activity

Have a class discussion about how Homeside Activities changed from the beginning to the end of the year. How did they get easier? How did they get harder? What did students do to help make the Homeside Activities successful? What did parents or adult friends do to help make the activities successful? What were some favorite Homeside Activities? Explain this final Homeside Activity, and send home students' Homeside Activity folders along with it.

Follow-Up

Invite volunteers to tell about the Homeside Activities they created. Students might also enjoy making a Homeside Handbook for future students, with suggestions for making Homeside Activities successful. Or, they might enjoy compiling a class book about Homeside Highlights that can be reproduced and taken home by students at the end of the school year so that they can share with each other the wisdom, experiences, and knowledge contributed by classmates' family members and friends. (If you reproduce actual finished Homeside Activities for this book, check with parents before sharing their contributions; an alternative would be to have students write about what they consider the Homeside Activity highlights and what they learned from them.)

Homeside Activities in Review

Dear Student,

You are in charge of this Homeside Activity, which means you are in charge of finding an adult to do it with you, finding time you both have free to do it, explaining and "directing" the activity, making sure the adult signs it, and bringing it back to class. Please find about 20 minutes that you can spend on the activity with a parent or other adult—a neighbor, grandparent, older brother or sister, or family friend. If you'd like, get a bunch of people involved!

One of the most important reasons for doing this activity is that you and the adult will learn things from each other about what you think, feel, know, and want to know. In class we can then also learn from each other, when we share what we have learned at home. Just be sure to ask the adults for permission to pass along what they say—and don't forget to thank them for contributing to our class's learning!

For this last Homeside Activity, talk with a parent or adult friend about some highlights of this year's Homeside Activities.

With the adult, look at the Homeside Activities from the entire year, and talk about the things you each did to make these activities successful.

Tell each other which Homeside Activities were your favorites. What did you like about these?

Then think of a topic or question for which you wish there were a Homeside Activity. Have a conversation about this topic.

On the back of this page, write a few sentences about the activity you created and what you and the adult discussed about it.

NOTES

My new Homeside Activity:

....
....
....
....

What we discussed about this topic:

....
....
....
....
....
....
....
....
....

....

Comments
....

After you have completed
this activity, each of you
please sign your name and
the date below. If you have
any comments, please
write them in the space
provided.

....
....
....
....
....

Signatures   **Date**

_____   _____   _____

Please return this activity to school. Thank you.

Les presentamos las Actividades Familiares

Querido alumno o querida alumna,

Tú eres la persona encargada de realizar esta Actividad Familiar: te toca encontrar a una persona mayor que la pueda hacer contigo, hallar un tiempo que los dos tengan libre, llevar a cabo la actividad, obtener la firma y por último traer la actividad de vuelta a la escuela. Necesitarás hallar unos 20 minutos que puedas dedicarle a la actividad junto con uno de tus padres o con otra persona mayor: pudiera ser un vecino o una vecina, uno de tus abuelitos, tu hermano o hermana mayor, o algún amigo o amiga de la familia. Si quieres, ¡puedes reunir a todo un grupo!

Una de las razones principales por la cual realizar esta actividad es que cada uno de ustedes aprenderá mucho acerca de la otra persona: ambos aprenderán qué piensa, qué siente, qué sabe y qué quiere saber cada cual. Más tarde en la clase, seguiremos aprendiendo unos de otros al compartir lo que hemos aprendido en casa. Sólo asegúrate de pedirles permiso a las personas mayores para compartir lo que te han contado, y ¡no te olvides de agradecerles por su contribución a nuestro aprendizaje!

Cuéntale a uno de tus padres o a otra persona mayor que este año escolar traerás a casa algunas Actividades Familiares.

Explícale que para realizar estas actividades, necesitarás conversar con él o con ella sobre algunos temas relacionados con tu trabajo escolar. Muéstrale a la persona mayor la carpeta que preparaste para tus Actividades Familiares, y háblale de tu diseño.

Conversen de cómo las Actividades Familiares serán distintas de otras tareas. Luego cada cual dirá qué es lo que quizá le guste de estas "tareas" de diálogo.

Escribe tus apuntes en el dorso de esta hoja.

MIS APUNTES

Las formas en que las Actividades Familiares serán distintas de otras tareas:

_____

_____

_____

_____

Las cosas que quizá le gusten a la persona mayor de estas tareas de diálogo:

_____

_____

_____

_____

Las cosas que quizá me gusten a mí de estas tareas de diálogo:

_____

_____

_____

_____

Comentarios

Después que hayan comple-
tado esta actividad, haga el
favor cada uno de firmar y
de escribir la fecha en el
lugar indicado. Si quisieran
hacer cualquier comentario,
por favor escríbanlo aquí.

_____

_____

_____

_____

Firmas

Fecha

_____ _____ _____

Por favor trae esta actividad devuelta a la escuela. Gracias.

Este año escolar

Querido alumno
o querida alumna,

Tú eres la persona encargada de realizar esta Actividad Familiar: te toca encontrar a una persona mayor que la pueda hacer contigo, hallar un tiempo que los dos tengan libre, llevar a cabo la actividad, obtener la firma y por último traer la actividad de vuelta a la escuela. Necesitarás hallar unos 20 minutos que puedas dedicarle a la actividad junto con uno de tus padres o con otra persona mayor: pudiera ser un vecino o una vecina, uno de tus abuelitos, tu hermano o hermana mayor, o algún amigo o amiga de la familia. Si quieres, ¡puedes reunir a todo un grupo!

Una de las razones principales por la cual realizar esta actividad es que cada uno de ustedes aprenderá mucho acerca de la otra persona: ambos aprenderán qué piensa, qué siente, qué sabe y qué quiere saber cada cual. Más tarde en la clase, seguiremos aprendiendo unos de otros al compartir lo que hemos aprendido en casa. Sólo asegúrate de pedirles permiso a las personas mayores para compartir lo que te han contado, y ¡no te olvides de agradecerles por su contribución a nuestro aprendizaje!

Cuéntale a uno de tus padres o a otra persona mayor cómo piensas que será este año escolar. ¿Qué crees que te va a gustar? ¿Qué crees que no te va a gustar?

Nombra tres cosas que quisieras aprender o en las que quisieras mejorar este año. Explica por qué piensas que lo que quieres aprender te resultará fácil o te resultará difícil.

Luego pregúntale a la persona mayor si hay alguna materia que le hubiera gustado aprender más a fondo cuando estaba en la escuela. Haz tus apuntes en el revés de esta hoja.

MIS APUNTES

Lo que pienso que me va a gustar de este año escolar:

....

....

Lo que pienso que no me va a gustar de este año escolar:

....

....

Tres cosas que quiero aprender o en las que quiero mejorar este año:

1 ....

....

2 ....

....

3 ....

....

Algo que a la persona mayor le hubiera gustado aprender más a fondo en la escuela:

....

....

....

Comentarios

Después que hayan comple-
tado esta actividad, haga el
favor cada uno de firmar y
de escribir la fecha en el
lugar indicado. Si quisieran
hacer cualquier comentario,
por favor escríbanlo aquí.

....

....

....

....

Firmas   **Fecha**

_____   _____   _____

Por favor trae esta actividad devuelta a la escuela. Gracias.

Matemáticas cotidianas

Querido alumno o querida alumna,

Tú eres la persona encargada de realizar esta Actividad Familiar: te toca encontrar a una persona mayor que la pueda hacer contigo, hallar un tiempo que los dos tengan libre, llevar a cabo la actividad, obtener la firma y por último traer la actividad de vuelta a la escuela. Necesitarás hallar unos 20 minutos que puedas dedicarle a la actividad junto con uno de tus padres o con otra persona mayor: pudiera ser un vecino o una vecina, uno de tus abuelitos, tu hermano o hermana mayor, o algún amigo o amiga de la familia. Si quieres, ¡puedes reunir a todo un grupo!

Una de las razones principales por la cual realizar esta actividad es que cada uno de ustedes aprenderá mucho acerca de la otra persona: ambos aprenderán qué piensa, qué siente, qué sabe y qué quiere saber cada cual. Más tarde en la clase, seguiremos aprendiendo unos de otros al compartir lo que hemos aprendido en casa. Sólo asegúrate de pedirles permiso a las personas mayores para compartir lo que te han contado, y ¡no te olvides de agradecerles por su contribución a nuestro aprendizaje!

Utiliza las preguntas que encontrarás en el dorso de esta hoja para entrevistar a un pariente o a otra persona mayor sobre cómo utiliza las matemáticas en la vida diaria. También averigua cómo la persona mayor aprendió las matemáticas cuando estaba en la escuela. Si quieres, puedes añadir tus propias preguntas a la entrevista. Escribe tus apuntes en los lugares indicados.

PREGUNTAS PARA LA ENTREVISTA:

¿Puedes pensar en dos o tres maneras en que utilizas las matemáticas en tus actividades diarias?

....

....

....

....

¿Conoces algunos "trucos" que utilizas para calcular más rápidamente? Si conoces algunos, ¿me los puedes explicar?

....

....

....

....

Cuéntame un relato de cuando eras pequeño y estabas aprendiendo las matemáticas en la escuela.

....

....

....

....

....

Comentarios

Después que hayan completado esta actividad, haga el favor cada uno de firmar y de escribir la fecha en el lugar indicado. Si quisieran hacer cualquier comentario, por favor escríbanlo aquí.

....

....

....

....

Firmas   **Fecha**

_____   _____   _____

Por favor trae esta actividad devuelta a la escuela. Gracias.

Una presentación de poesía

Querido alumno o querida alumna,

Tú eres la persona encargada de realizar esta Actividad Familiar: te toca encontrar a una persona mayor que la pueda hacer contigo, hallar un tiempo que los dos tengan libre, llevar a cabo la actividad, obtener la firma y por último traer la actividad de vuelta a la escuela. Necesitarás hallar unos 20 minutos que puedas dedicarle a la actividad junto con uno de tus padres o con otra persona mayor: pudiera ser un vecino o una vecina, uno de tus abuelitos, tu hermano o hermana mayor, o algún amigo o amiga de la familia. Si quieres, ¡puedes reunir a todo un grupo!

Una de las razones principales por la cual realizar esta actividad es que cada uno de ustedes aprenderá mucho acerca de la otra persona: ambos aprenderán qué piensa, qué siente, qué sabe y qué quiere saber cada cual. Más tarde en la clase, seguiremos aprendiendo unos de otros al compartir lo que hemos aprendido en casa. Sólo asegúrate de pedirles permiso a las personas mayores para compartir lo que te han contado, y ¡no te olvides de agradecerles por su contribución a nuestro aprendizaje!

Presenta el poema que has elegido a uno de tus padres o a otra persona mayor.

Cuéntale por qué elegiste ese poema. Subraya dos o tres de tus renglones o frases favoritas, y explica por qué te gustan.

Luego pídele a la persona mayor que subraye dos o tres de sus renglones o frases favoritas. Conversen sobre lo que cada cual eligió, y comparen sus elecciones. Escribe tus apuntes en el dorso de esta hoja.

MIS APUNTES

La parte del poema que más me gusta, y por qué me gusta:

_____

_____

_____

_____

_____

_____

La parte del poema que más le gusta a la persona mayor, y por qué le gusta:

_____

_____

_____

_____

_____

_____

Comentarios

Después que hayan comple-
tado esta actividad, haga el
favor cada uno de firmar y
de escribir la fecha en el
lugar indicado. Si quisieran
hacer cualquier comentario,
por favor escríbanlo aquí.

_____

_____

_____

_____

Firmas   **Fecha**

_____ _____   _____

Por favor trae esta actividad devuelta a la escuela. Gracias.

Mi opinión

Querido alumno o querida alumna,

Tú eres la persona encargada de realizar esta Actividad Familiar: te toca encontrar a una persona mayor que la pueda hacer contigo, hallar un tiempo que los dos tengan libre, llevar a cabo la actividad, obtener la firma y por último traer la actividad de vuelta a la escuela. Necesitarás hallar unos 20 minutos que puedas dedicarle a la actividad junto con uno de tus padres o con otra persona mayor: pudiera ser un vecino o una vecina, uno de tus abuelitos, tu hermano o hermana mayor, o algún amigo o amiga de la familia. Si quieres, ¡puedes reunir a todo un grupo!

Una de las razones principales por la cual realizar esta actividad es que cada uno de ustedes aprenderá mucho acerca de la otra persona: ambos aprenderán qué piensa, qué siente, qué sabe y qué quiere saber cada cual. Más tarde en la clase, seguiremos aprendiendo unos de otros al compartir lo que hemos aprendido en casa. Sólo asegúrate de pedirles permiso a las personas mayores para compartir lo que te han contado, y ¡no te olvides de agradecerles por su contribución a nuestro aprendizaje!

Háblale a uno de tus padres o a otra persona mayor de un tema que te inquieta. Explícale por qué te interesa ese tema, y por qué le escribiste a la persona o a la publicación que elegiste.

Luego léele tu carta a la persona mayor. Pregúntale qué opiniones tiene sobre el tema.

Conversen sobre las maneras en que las ideas de ambos se parecen, y las maneras en que se diferencian. Escribe tus apuntes en dorso de esta hoja.

Las maneras en que nuestras ideas
se parecen

Las maneras en que nuestras ideas
se diferencian

Comentarios

Después que hayan comple-
tado esta actividad, haga el
favor cada uno de firmar y
de escribir la fecha en el
lugar indicado. Si quisieran
hacer cualquier comentario,
por favor escríbanlo aquí.

Firmas

Fecha

Por favor trae esta actividad devuelta a la escuela. Gracias.

Antes y ahora

Querido alumno o querida alumna,

Tú eres la persona encargada de realizar esta Actividad Familiar: te toca encontrar a una persona mayor que la pueda hacer contigo, hallar un tiempo que los dos tengan libre, llevar a cabo la actividad, obtener la firma y por último traer la actividad de vuelta a la escuela. Necesitarás hallar unos 20 minutos que puedas dedicarle a la actividad junto con uno de tus padres o con otra persona mayor: pudiera ser un vecino o una vecina, uno de tus abuelitos, tu hermano o hermana mayor, o algún amigo o amiga de la familia. Si quieres, ¡puedes reunir a todo un grupo!

Una de las razones principales por la cual realizar esta actividad es que cada uno de ustedes aprenderá mucho acerca de la otra persona: ambos aprenderán qué piensa, qué siente, qué sabe y qué quiere saber cada cual. Más tarde en la clase, seguiremos aprendiendo unos de otros al compartir lo que hemos aprendido en casa. Sólo asegúrate de pedirles permiso a las personas mayores para compartir lo que te han contado, y ¡no te olvides de agradecerles por su contribución a nuestro aprendizaje!

Lee el poema "Los huesos de la abuela" con un familiar o con otra persona mayor. Utiliza las preguntas que encontrarás al dorso de esta hoja para entrevistar a la persona mayor sobre la música, los bailes y los estilos que estaban de moda cuando esa persona tenía tu edad.

Si quieres, agrega tus propias preguntas a la entrevista. Anota tus apuntes en el espacio correspondiente. En clase, utilizaremos estos apuntes para un ejercicio escrito.

ACTIVIDAD FAMILIAR

Los huesos de la abuela

La abuela creció
en los años 40
todavía sabe bailar el "jitterbug"
lo solían bailar
al ritmo de la música
de Duke Ellington,
Benny Carter, Count Basie
y otros.

Ella sabe hacer girar el yo-yó
mucho mejor que yo
y a veces se pone dos palos
que llama huesos
entre los nudillos
de los dedos y empieza:

tac tac tíqueti
tíqueti tac
tíqueti tíqueti tíqueti
tac tac
eh, tíqueti tac
eh, tíqueti tac
¡tac tac tíqueti
tíqueti tac!

—Eloise Greenfield*
(traducido por Malena Samaniego)

PREGUNTAS PARA LA ENTREVISTA

Cuando tenías mi edad, ¿cuáles eran tus grupos de música preferidos? ¿Por qué?

¿Cuáles eran los bailes que solías bailar?

¿Qué tipo de ropa y qué peinados estaban de moda en ese tiempo?

¿Qué otras cosas recuerdas que estaban muy de moda en esos días?

Comentarios

Después que hayan completado esta actividad, haga el favor cada uno de firmar y de escribir la fecha en el lugar indicado. Si quisieran hacer cualquier comentario, por favor escríbanlo aquí.

Firmas

Fecha

Por favor trae esta actividad devuelta a la escuela. Gracias.

Una cápsula personal del tiempo

Querido alumno o querida alumna,

Tú eres la persona encargada de realizar esta Actividad Familiar: te toca encontrar a una persona mayor que la pueda hacer contigo, hallar un tiempo que los dos tengan libre, llevar a cabo la actividad, obtener la firma y por último traer la actividad de vuelta a la escuela. Necesitarás hallar unos 20 minutos que puedas dedicarle a la actividad junto con uno de tus padres o con otra persona mayor: pudiera ser un vecino o una vecina, uno de tus abuelitos, tu hermano o hermana mayor, o algún amigo o amiga de la familia. Si quieres, ¡puedes reunir a todo un grupo!

Una de las razones principales por la cual realizar esta actividad es que cada uno de ustedes aprenderá mucho acerca de la otra persona: ambos aprenderán qué piensa, qué siente, qué sabe y qué quiere saber cada cual. Más tarde en la clase, seguiremos aprendiendo unos de otros al compartir lo que hemos aprendido en casa. Sólo asegúrate de pedirles permiso a las personas mayores para compartir lo que te han contado, y ¡no te olvides de agradecerles por su contribución a nuestro aprendizaje!

En el dorso de esta hoja, escribe de 5 a 10 cosas que incluirías en una cápsula personal del tiempo que fuera a abrirse en 25 años. Escoge cosas que cuenten algo acerca de ti y de lo que te gusta.

Cuéntale a uno de tus padres o a otra persona mayor sobre las cosas que has elegido, y por qué las incluirías en tu cápsula del tiempo. ¿Qué nos cuenta cada objeto de ti?

Pregúntale a la persona mayor si hay algún otro objeto que él o que ella añadiría para dar una perspectiva más completa de quién eres tú. Apunta sus ideas en el revés de esta hoja.

Lo que yo escogí para mi cápsula del tiempo   Las cosas que añadió la persona mayor

....

....

....

....

....

....

....

....

....

....

....

Comentarios

Después que hayan comple-
tado esta actividad, haga el
favor cada uno de firmar y
de escribir la fecha en el
lugar indicado. Si quisieran
hacer cualquier comentario,
por favor escríbanlo aquí.

....

....

....

....

Firmas   **Fecha**

_____   _____   _____

Por favor trae esta actividad devuelta a la escuela. Gracias.

Camina bien erguido

**Querido alumno
o querida alumna,**

Tú eres la persona encargada de realizar esta Actividad Familiar: te toca encontrar a una persona mayor que la pueda hacer contigo, hallar un tiempo que los dos tengan libre, llevar a cabo la actividad, obtener la firma y por último traer la actividad de vuelta a la escuela. Necesitarás hallar unos 20 minutos que puedas dedicarle a la actividad junto con uno de tus padres o con otra persona mayor: pudiera ser un vecino o una vecina, uno de tus abuelitos, tu hermano o hermana mayor, o algún amigo o amiga de la familia. Si quieres, ¡puedes reunir a todo un grupo!

Una de las razones principales por la cual realizar esta actividad es que cada uno de ustedes aprenderá mucho acerca de la otra persona: ambos aprenderán qué piensa, qué siente, qué sabe y qué quiere saber cada cual. Más tarde en la clase, seguiremos aprendiendo unos de otros al compartir lo que hemos aprendido en casa. Sólo asegúrate de pedirles permiso a las personas mayores para compartir lo que te han contado, y ¡no te olvides de agradecerles por su contribución a nuestro aprendizaje!

Lee el poema "Enero" con uno de tus padres o con alguna otra persona mayor.

Conversen sobre lo que piensan que quiere decir "camina bien erguido por el mundo". ¿Por qué creen que la madre da este consejo al comienzo de un año nuevo?

Hagan una lista, en el dorso de esta hoja, de las razones que tiene cada uno de ustedes para caminar bien erguido o para caminar bien erguida. Pueden turnarse para ofrecerle razones a la otra persona para su lista. Sólo escriban una razón si los dos están de acuerdo con ella.

Enero

—Camina bien erguido por el mundo
—le dice Mamá
a Everett Anderson—.
El año está nuevito
y los días también.
Camina bien erguido por el mundo
—le dice.

> —Lucille Clifton*
> traducido por Rosa Zubizarreta

* From *Everett Anderson's Year* by Lucille Clifton. Copyright © 1978 by Lucille Clifton. Reprinted by permission of Henry Holt & Co., Inc.

Las razones que tengo para caminar bien erguido o bien erguida:

....

....

....

....

....

....

....

....

....

....

....

....

Las razones que tiene la persona mayor para caminar bien erguido o bien erguida:

....

....

....

....

....

....

....

....

....

....

....

....

Comentarios

Después que hayan completado esta actividad, haga el favor cada uno de firmar y de escribir la fecha en el lugar indicado. Si quisieran hacer cualquier comentario, por favor escríbanlo aquí.

....

....

....

....

Firmas

Fecha

_____ _____ _____

Por favor trae esta actividad devuelta a la escuela. Gracias.

Tradiciones familiares

Querido alumno o querida alumna,

Tú eres la persona encargada de realizar esta Actividad Familiar: te toca encontrar a una persona mayor que la pueda hacer contigo, hallar un tiempo que los dos tengan libre, llevar a cabo la actividad, obtener la firma y por último traer la actividad de vuelta a la escuela. Necesitarás hallar unos 20 minutos que puedas dedicarle a la actividad junto con uno de tus padres o con otra persona mayor: pudiera ser un vecino o una vecina, uno de tus abuelitos, tu hermano o hermana mayor, o algún amigo o amiga de la familia. Si quieres, ¡puedes reunir a todo un grupo!

Una de las razones principales por la cual realizar esta actividad es que cada uno de ustedes aprenderá mucho acerca de la otra persona: ambos aprenderán qué piensa, qué siente, qué sabe y qué quiere saber cada cual. Más tarde en la clase, seguiremos aprendiendo unos de otros al compartir lo que hemos aprendido en casa. Sólo asegúrate de pedirles permiso a las personas mayores para compartir lo que te han contado, y ¡no te olvides de agradecerles por su contribución a nuestro aprendizaje!

Entrevista a uno de tus padres o a alguna otra persona mayor sobre la historia de tu familia. Pregúntale a la persona mayor una o varias de las siguientes preguntas (es posible que la persona mayor no tenga relatos que contar sobre cada pregunta, pero seguramente tendrá relatos sobre algunas de ellas). Luego escribe en el dorso de esta hoja un resumen de uno de los relatos que te gustaría compartir con la clase.

PREGUNTAS PARA LA ENTREVISTA:

- ¿Hay un relato sobre algún personaje de la familia que me pudieras contar?

- ¿Conoces un relato sobre cómo empezó un chiste familiar o un dicho familiar?

- ¿Me puedes contar un relato sobre un matrimonio familiar, o sobre cómo se conoció una pareja de la familia?

- ¿Cuál es tu relato favorito de cuando eras pequeño o de cuando eras pequeña?

RELATO DE UNA TRADICIÓN O DE UN ACONTECIMIENTO FAMILIAR

Escribe aquí un resumen de uno de los relatos que te contaron en la entrevista.

....

....

....

....

....

....

....

....

....

....

....

....

....

Comentarios

Después que hayan comple-
tado esta actividad, haga el
favor cada uno de firmar y
de escribir la fecha en el
lugar indicado. Si quisieran
hacer cualquier comentario,
por favor escríbanlo aquí.

Firmas   **Fecha**

_____   _____   _____

Por favor trae esta actividad devuelta a la escuela. Gracias.

Harvey

Harvey no se ríe de cómo yo me quedo bajito mientras los demás siguen creciendo.

Harvey se acuerda de que me gustan los "jellybeans"—menos los negros.

Harvey me presta una camisa sin preguntarme cuándo la devuelvo.

Le tengo miedo a los fantasmas pero sólo a Harvey se lo digo.

Harvey piensa que sí cuando le digo que algún día me casaré con Margie Rose.

Harvey comparte su limonada conmigo—trago por trago.

Me recuerda en voz baja cuando me olvido de cerrar la cremallera.

Me asegura que no tengo deformes los dedos de los pies, por cierto que no.

Harvey me llama por teléfono cuando estoy en cama, mal de la garganta y con un resfrío.

Harvey dice que soy amable—pero no demasiado amable.

Y si hay un tren con rumbo al paraíso

no me subiré en él si no es con Harvey. Iremos juntos.

—Judith Viorst*
traducido por Rosa Zubizarreta

Harvey

Querido alumno o querida alumna,

Tú eres la persona encargada de realizar esta Actividad Familiar: te toca encontrar a una persona mayor que la pueda hacer contigo, hallar un tiempo que los dos tengan libre, llevar a cabo la actividad, obtener la firma y por último traer la actividad de vuelta a la escuela. Necesitarás hallar unos 20 minutos que puedas dedicarle a la actividad junto con uno de tus padres o con otra persona mayor: pudiera ser un vecino o una vecina, uno de tus abuelitos, tu hermano o hermana mayor, o algún amigo o amiga de la familia. Si quieres, ¡puedes reunir a todo un grupo!

Una de las razones principales por la cual realizar esta actividad es que cada uno de ustedes aprenderá mucho acerca de la otra persona: ambos aprenderán qué piensa, qué siente, qué sabe y qué quiere saber cada cual. Más tarde en la clase, seguiremos aprendiendo unos de otros al compartir lo que hemos aprendido en casa. Sólo asegúrate de pedirles permiso a las personas mayores para compartir lo que te han contado, y ¡no te olvides de agradecerles por su contribución a nuestro aprendizaje!

En el poema "Harvey," una persona nos describe cómo es su amigo especial con uno de tus padres o con otra persona mayor. Lee el poema que se encuentra en el revés de esta hoja. Compartan sus ideas sobre por qué Harvey es un buen amigo.

Luego, utilicen las preguntas que encontrarán al dorso de esta hoja para que ambos se entrevisten acerca de las amistades. Escribe tus apuntes en los lugares indicados.

PREGUNTAS PARA LA ENTREVISTA

¿Qué cualidades tiene Harvey que piensas que te gustaría encontrar en un amigo o en una amiga?

la persona joven:

....

....

....

la persona mayor:

....

....

....

¿Qué cualidades son de mayor importancia para ti en un buen amigo?

la persona joven:

....

....

....

la persona mayor:

....

....

....

(Sólo para la persona mayor) ¿Recuerdas a un buen amigo o a una buena amiga que tuviste cuando eras pequeño o cuando eras pequeña? ¿Por qué recuerdas a esa persona?

....

....

....

¿Quién es un buen amigo tuyo o una buena amiga tuya ahora? ¿Por qué es esa persona importante para ti? ¿Por qué le eres importante tú a esa persona?

la persona joven:

....

....

....

....

la persona mayor:

....

....

....

....

Comentarios

Después que hayan completado esta actividad, haga el favor cada uno de firmar y de escribir la fecha en el lugar indicado. Si quisieran hacer cualquier comentario, por favor escríbanlo aquí.

....

....

....

....

....

....

Firmas

Fecha

_____   _____   _____

Por favor trae esta actividad devuelta a la escuela. Gracias.

Intercambiemos lugares

Querido alumno o querida alumna,

Tú eres la persona encargada de realizar esta Actividad Familiar: te toca encontrar a una persona mayor que la pueda hacer contigo, hallar un tiempo que los dos tengan libre, llevar a cabo la actividad, obtener la firma y por último traer la actividad de vuelta a la escuela. Necesitarás hallar unos 20 minutos que puedas dedicarle a la actividad junto con uno de tus padres o con otra persona mayor: pudiera ser un vecino o una vecina, uno de tus abuelitos, tu hermano o hermana mayor, o algún amigo o amiga de la familia. Si quieres, ¡puedes reunir a todo un grupo!

Una de las razones principales por la cual realizar esta actividad es que cada uno de ustedes aprenderá mucho acerca de la otra persona: ambos aprenderán qué piensa, qué siente, qué sabe y qué quiere saber cada cual. Más tarde en la clase, seguiremos aprendiendo unos de otros al compartir lo que hemos aprendido en casa. Sólo asegúrate de pedirles permiso a las personas mayores para compartir lo que te han contado, y ¡no te olvides de agradecerles por su contribución a nuestro aprendizaje!

Cuando leemos cuentos y novelas en la clase, muchas veces conversamos sobre cómo se vería la vida desde el punto de vista de uno u otro personaje.

Para esta Actividad Familiar, cuéntale a uno de tus familiares o a alguna amistad de la familia sobre algún personaje con el cual te gustaría intercambiar lugares por un día. ¿Por qué te gustaría ser esa persona? ¿Cómo crees que esa persona se sentiría de estar en tu lugar por un día?

Luego dale la oportunidad a la persona mayor de hablar acerca de un personaje (o de una persona real) con quien le gustaría intercambiar lugares por un día. Escribe tus apuntes sobre la conversación en el dorso de esta hoja.

MIS APUNTES

El personaje con el cual me gustaría intercambiar lugares:

la persona joven:

....

....

....

la persona mayor:

....

....

....

La razón por la cual me gustaría intercambiar lugares con este personaje:

la persona joven:

....

....

....

la persona mayor:

....

....

....

Lo que ese personaje sentiría al estar en mi lugar por un día:

la persona joven:

....

....

....

la persona mayor:

....

....

....

Comentarios

Después que hayan completado esta actividad, haga el favor cada uno de firmar y de escribir la fecha en el lugar indicado. Si quisieran hacer cualquier comentario, por favor escríbanlo aquí.

....

....

....

....

....

Firmas   **Fecha**

_____   _____   _____

Por favor trae esta actividad devuelta a la escuela. Gracias.

Cortaron tres árboles

Querido alumno
o querida alumna,

Tú eres la persona encargada de realizar esta Actividad Familiar: te toca encontrar a una persona mayor que la pueda hacer contigo, hallar un tiempo que los dos tengan libre, llevar a cabo la actividad, obtener la firma y por último traer la actividad de vuelta a la escuela. Necesitarás hallar unos 20 minutos que puedas dedicarle a la actividad junto con uno de tus padres o con otra persona mayor: pudiera ser un vecino o una vecina, uno de tus abuelitos, tu hermano o hermana mayor, o algún amigo o amiga de la familia. Si quieres, ¡puedes reunir a todo un grupo!

Una de las razones principales por la cual realizar esta actividad es que cada uno de ustedes aprenderá mucho acerca de la otra persona: ambos aprenderán qué piensa, qué siente, qué sabe y qué quiere saber cada cual. Más tarde en la clase, seguiremos aprendiendo unos de otros al compartir lo que hemos aprendido en casa. Sólo asegúrate de pedirles permiso a las personas mayores para compartir lo que te han contado, y ¡no te olvides de agradecerles por su contribución a nuestro aprendizaje!

Cuéntale a uno de tus padres o a otra persona mayor algo sobre las preocupaciones ambientales que tu clase está estudiando. Luego léele este poema.

Conversen de los sentimientos que piensan que el poema expresa sobre los tres árboles cortados. Luego conversen sobre cómo se siente cada uno de ustedes cuando cortan árboles. Haz una lista de esos sentimientos en el revés de esta hoja.

Cortaron tres árboles

—A Ernesto Halffter

Eran tres.
(Vino el día con sus hachas.)
Eran dos.
(Alas rastreras de plata.)
Era uno.
Era ninguno.
(Se quedó desnuda el agua.)

—Federico García Lorca*

* "They Cut Down Three Trees" by Federico García Lorca from *The Cricket Sings* by Federico García Lorca, © 1980 published by New Directions.

Cómo se siente la persona mayor cuando cortan árboles

Cómo me siento yo cuando cortan árboles

Comentarios

Después que hayan completado esta actividad, haga el favor cada uno de firmar y de escribir la fecha en el lugar indicado. Si quisieran hacer cualquier comentario, por favor escríbanlo aquí.

Firmas

Fecha

Por favor trae esta actividad devuelta a la escuela. Gracias.

La primavera

Querido alumno o querida alumna,

Tú eres la persona encargada de realizar esta Actividad Familiar: te toca encontrar a una persona mayor que la pueda hacer contigo, hallar un tiempo que los dos tengan libre, llevar a cabo la actividad, obtener la firma y por último traer la actividad de vuelta a la escuela. Necesitarás hallar unos 20 minutos que puedas dedicarle a la actividad junto con uno de tus padres o con otra persona mayor: pudiera ser un vecino o una vecina, uno de tus abuelitos, tu hermano o hermana mayor, o algún amigo o amiga de la familia. Si quieres, ¡puedes reunir a todo un grupo!

Una de las razones principales por la cual realizar esta actividad es que cada uno de ustedes aprenderá mucho acerca de la otra persona: ambos aprenderán qué piensa, qué siente, qué sabe y qué quiere saber cada cual. Más tarde en la clase, seguiremos aprendiendo unos de otros al compartir lo que hemos aprendido en casa. Sólo asegúrate de pedirles permiso a las personas mayores para compartir lo que te han contado, y ¡no te olvides de agradecerles por su contribución a nuestro aprendizaje!

Cuéntale a uno de tus padres o a otra persona mayor de tu dibujo de la primavera. Cuéntale también de lo que más disfrutas de la primavera y de lo que esperas poder hacer en esta temporada. Usa los apuntes que has escrito en el dorso de esta hoja para ayudarte a expresar tus ideas.

Luego pídele a la persona mayor que te cuente qué disfruta de la primavera y qué cosas espera hacer en este tiempo. Escribe tus apuntes en el revés de esta hoja.

MIS APUNTES

Lo que significa mi dibujo de la primavera:

_____

_____

Lo que yo disfruto de la primavera, y por qué lo disfruto:

_____

_____

Lo que estoy esperando hacer en la primavera, y por qué:

_____

_____

Lo que la persona mayor disfruta de la primavera, y por qué lo disfruta:

_____

_____

Lo que la persona mayor está esperando hacer en la primavera, y por qué:

_____

_____

Comentarios

Después que hayan comple-
tado esta actividad, haga el
favor cada uno de firmar y
de escribir la fecha en el
lugar indicado. Si quisieran
hacer cualquier comentario,
por favor escríbanlo aquí.

_____

_____

_____

_____

Firmas   **Fecha**

_____ _____   _____

Por favor trae esta actividad devuelta a la escuela. Gracias.

El trabajo en conjunto

Querido alumno
o querida alumna,

Tú eres la persona encargada de realizar esta Actividad Familiar: te toca encontrar a una persona mayor que la pueda hacer contigo, hallar un tiempo que los dos tengan libre, llevar a cabo la actividad, obtener la firma y por último traer la actividad de vuelta a la escuela. Necesitarás hallar unos 20 minutos que puedas dedicarle a la actividad junto con uno de tus padres o con otra persona mayor: pudiera ser un vecino o una vecina, uno de tus abuelitos, tu hermano o hermana mayor, o algún amigo o amiga de la familia. Si quieres, ¡puedes reunir a todo un grupo!

Una de las razones principales por la cual realizar esta actividad es que cada uno de ustedes aprenderá mucho acerca de la otra persona: ambos aprenderán qué piensa, qué siente, qué sabe y qué quiere saber cada cual. Más tarde en la clase, seguiremos aprendiendo unos de otros al compartir lo que hemos aprendido en casa. Sólo asegúrate de pedirles permiso a las personas mayores para compartir lo que te han contado, y ¡no te olvides de agradecerles por su contribución a nuestro aprendizaje!

Cuéntale a uno de tus padres o a otra persona mayor sobre un proyecto de grupo en el cual has participado en la clase. Luego pregúntale a la persona mayor de alguna vez en que ha trabajado en grupo con otras personas para llevar a cabo un trabajo. Por ejemplo, cada cual pudiera relatar sus ideas sobre los siguientes temas:

- lo más útil de trabajar en conjunto con otros

- lo más difícil de trabajar en conjunto con otros

- los problemas que tuvo el grupo de cada cual, y cómo los resolvieron

Juntos, anoten en el dorso de esta hoja los "beneficios" (cosas buenas) y las "desventajas" (cosas difíciles) del trabajo en grupo.

Los beneficios de trabajar en grupo

Las desventajas de trabajar en grupo

Comentarios

Después que hayan completado esta actividad, haga el favor cada uno de firmar y de escribir la fecha en el lugar indicado. Si quisieran hacer cualquier comentario, por favor escríbanlo aquí.

Firmas

Fecha

Por favor trae esta actividad devuelta a la escuela. Gracias.

Discurso para los jóvenes

Diles,
diles a quienes lo ven todo mal,
a quienes abofetean al sol,
a quienes ensucian el ser,
a quienes silencian la armonía:
—Aun si no estás listo para que llegue el día,
no puede seguir siendo siempre de noche.
Estarás en lo cierto.
Porque ése es el jonrón más difícil.

Vive, no para las batallas que ganes.
Vive, no para el fin de la canción.
Vive, a lo largo del son.

—Gwendolyn Brooks*
traducido por Rosa Zubizarreta

MIS APUNTES

Lo que nosotros pensamos que significa el poema:

Nuestros consejos para la gente joven:

Discurso para los jóvenes

Querido alumno o querida alumna,

Tú eres la persona encargada de realizar esta Actividad Familiar: te toca encontrar a una persona mayor que la pueda hacer contigo, hallar un tiempo que los dos tengan libre, llevar a cabo la actividad, obtener la firma y por último traer la actividad de vuelta a la escuela. Necesitarás hallar unos 20 minutos que puedas dedicarle a la actividad junto con uno de tus padres o con otra persona mayor: pudiera ser un vecino o una vecina, uno de tus abuelitos, tu hermano o hermana mayor, o algún amigo o amiga de la familia. Si quieres, ¡puedes reunir a todo un grupo!

Una de las razones principales por la cual realizar esta actividad es que cada uno de ustedes aprenderá mucho acerca de la otra persona: ambos aprenderán qué piensa, qué siente, qué sabe y qué quiere saber cada cual. Más tarde en la clase, seguiremos aprendiendo unos de otros al compartir lo que hemos aprendido en casa. Sólo asegúrate de pedirles permiso a las personas mayores para compartir lo que te han contado, y ¡no te olvides de agradecerles por su contribución a nuestro aprendizaje!

Lee el poema "Discurso para los jóvenes" con uno de tus padres o con otra persona mayor.

Conversa con la persona mayor sobre lo que crees que significa el poema. Hablen de qué consejos le darías tú a la gente joven. (Pueden estar de acuerdo o no sobre qué es lo importante.) Si quieres, escribe unos apuntes breves en la hoja adjunto.

Utiliza las ideas de tu conversación para escribir tu propio "Discurso para los jóvenes" en el revés de esta hoja.

Mi propio 'Discurso para los jóvenes'

Comentarios

Después que hayan completado esta actividad, haga el favor cada uno de firmar y de escribir la fecha en el lugar indicado. Si quisieran hacer cualquier comentario, por favor escríbanlo aquí.

Firmas

Fecha

Por favor trae esta actividad devuelta a la escuela. Gracias.

Montaje del año escolar

Querido alumno o querida alumna,

Tú eres la persona encargada de realizar esta Actividad Familiar: te toca encontrar a una persona mayor que la pueda hacer contigo, hallar un tiempo que los dos tengan libre, llevar a cabo la actividad, obtener la firma y por último traer la actividad de vuelta a la escuela. Necesitarás hallar unos 20 minutos que puedas dedicarle a la actividad junto con uno de tus padres o con otra persona mayor: pudiera ser un vecino o una vecina, uno de tus abuelitos, tu hermano o hermana mayor, o algún amigo o amiga de la familia. Si quieres, ¡puedes reunir a todo un grupo!

Una de las razones principales por la cual realizar esta actividad es que cada uno de ustedes aprenderá mucho acerca de la otra persona: ambos aprenderán qué piensa, qué siente, qué sabe y qué quiere saber cada cual. Más tarde en la clase, seguiremos aprendiendo unos de otros al compartir lo que hemos aprendido en casa. Sólo asegúrate de pedirles permiso a las personas mayores para compartir lo que te han contado, y ¡no te olvides de agradecerles por su contribución a nuestro aprendizaje!

Muestra a uno de tus padres o a otra persona mayor el montaje que has hecho sobre el año escolar. Conversen sobre las palabras y las imágenes que has incluido en tu montaje.

Usa los apuntes que has escrito en el dorso de esta hoja para ayudarte a hablar sobre tu montaje: lo que muestra de tus experiencias, de los acontecimientos especiales del año, de tus proyectos o materias favoritos, de lo que has aprendido acerca de ti mismo y acerca de los demás.

Luego pídele a la persona mayor que te ayude a contestar la última parte, que pregunta qué es lo que la persona mayor ha aprendido acerca de ti en este año.

MIS APUNTES PARA LA CONVERSACIÓN QUE TENDRÉ EN CASA

Algunas ideas acerca de mi montaje:

....

....

Lo que aprendí de un proyecto especial o en una de mis materias:

....

....

Algo que aprendí acerca de las personas este año:

....

....

Algo que aprendí acerca de mí mismo este año:

....

....

PREGUNTA PARA LA ENTREVISTA

Después que converses con la persona mayor sobre tu montaje, pídele que escriba o que te dicte una o dos oraciones sobre "algo que la persona mayor aprendió acerca de mí este año". Escriban las oraciones en el espacio a continuación.

....

....

....

....

Comentarios

Después que hayan completado esta actividad, haga el favor cada uno de firmar y de escribir la fecha en el lugar indicado. Si quisieran hacer cualquier comentario, por favor escríbanlo aquí.

....

....

....

....

Firmas   **Fecha**

_____   _____   _____

Por favor trae esta actividad devuelta a la escuela. Gracias.

Resumen de fin de año

Querido alumno o querida alumna,

Tú eres la persona encargada de realizar esta Actividad Familiar: te toca encontrar a una persona mayor que la pueda hacer contigo, hallar un tiempo que los dos tengan libre, llevar a cabo la actividad, obtener la firma y por último traer la actividad de vuelta a la escuela. Necesitarás hallar unos 20 minutos que puedas dedicarle a la actividad junto con uno de tus padres o con otra persona mayor: pudiera ser un vecino o una vecina, uno de tus abuelitos, tu hermano o hermana mayor, o algún amigo o amiga de la familia. Si quieres, ¡puedes reunir a todo un grupo!

Una de las razones principales por la cual realizar esta actividad es que cada uno de ustedes aprenderá mucho acerca de la otra persona: ambos aprenderán qué piensa, qué siente, qué sabe y qué quiere saber cada cual. Más tarde en la clase, seguiremos aprendiendo unos de otros al compartir lo que hemos aprendido en casa. Sólo asegúrate de pedirles permiso a las personas mayores para compartir lo que te han contado, y ¡no te olvides de agradecerles por su contribución a nuestro aprendizaje!

Conversa con uno de tus padres o con otra persona mayor sobre el año escolar que estás completando. Conversen de tus recuerdos favoritos y menos favoritos de este año.

Luego averigua cuáles son algunas de las cosas que la persona mayor recuerda de tu año escolar. ¿Cuál es el recuerdo favorito de él o de ella? Escribe tus apuntes en el dorso de esta hoja.

MIS APUNTES

Mis recuerdos favoritos de este año escolar:

....

....

....

....

Mis recuerdos menos favoritos de este año escolar:

....

....

....

....

Los recuerdos favoritos de la persona mayor de mi año escolar:

....

....

....

....

....

Comentarios

Después que hayan comple-
tado esta actividad, haga el
favor cada uno de firmar y
de escribir la fecha en el
lugar indicado. Si quisieran
hacer cualquier comentario,
por favor escríbanlo aquí.

Firmas   **Fecha**

Por favor trae esta actividad devuelta a la escuela. Gracias.

Repasemos las Actividades Familiares

Querido alumno o querida alumna,

Tú eres la persona encargada de realizar esta Actividad Familiar: te toca encontrar a una persona mayor que la pueda hacer contigo, hallar un tiempo que los dos tengan libre, llevar a cabo la actividad, obtener la firma y por último traer la actividad de vuelta a la escuela. Necesitarás hallar unos 20 minutos que puedas dedicarle a la actividad junto con uno de tus padres o con otra persona mayor: pudiera ser un vecino o una vecina, uno de tus abuelitos, tu hermano o hermana mayor, o algún amigo o amiga de la familia. Si quieres, ¡puedes reunir a todo un grupo!

Una de las razones principales por la cual realizar esta actividad es que cada uno de ustedes aprenderá mucho acerca de la otra persona: ambos aprenderán qué piensa, qué siente, qué sabe y qué quiere saber cada cual. Más tarde en la clase, seguiremos aprendiendo unos de otros al compartir lo que hemos aprendido en casa. Sólo asegúrate de pedirles permiso a las personas mayores para compartir lo que te han contado, y ¡no te olvides de agradecerles por su contribución a nuestro aprendizaje!

Para esta última Actividad Familiar, conversa con uno de tus padres o con otra persona mayor acerca de algunos de los momentos especiales que hayan tenido este año con las Actividades Familiares.

Repasen juntos las Actividades Familiares de todo el año, y conversen sobre qué hizo cada cual para asegurar el éxito de las actividades.

Hablen sobre las actividades favoritas de cada uno de ustedes. ¿Qué fue lo que les gustó de esas actividades?

Luego piensa en un tema o en una pregunta que te gustaría explorar en una Actividad Familiar. Conversen sobre ese tema. En el dorso de esta hoja, escribe algunas oraciones acerca de esta nueva Actividad Familiar que acabas de crear, y de la conversación que han tenido sobre ese tema.

MIS APUNTES

Mi nueva Actividad Familiar:

_____

_____

_____

_____

Lo que conversamos acerca de este tema:

_____

_____

_____

_____

_____

_____

_____

_____

Comentarios

Después que hayan comple-
tado esta actividad, haga el
favor cada uno de firmar y
de escribir la fecha en el
lugar indicado. Si quisieran
hacer cualquier comentario,
por favor escríbanlo aquí.

_____

_____

_____

_____

Firmas   **Fecha**

_____   _____   _____

Por favor trae esta actividad devuelta a la escuela. Gracias.

Funding for Developmental Studies Center has been generously provided by:

The Annenberg Foundation, Inc.

The Atlantic Philanthropies (USA) Inc.

The Robert Bowne Foundation, Inc.

The Annie E. Casey Foundation

Center for Substance Abuse Prevention:
    Substance Abuse and Mental Health Services Agency,
    U.S. Department of Health and Human Services

The Danforth Foundation

The DuBarry Foundation

The Ford Foundation

William T. Grant Foundation

Evelyn and Walter Haas, Jr. Fund

Walter and Elise Haas Fund

J. David and Pamela Hakman Family Foundation

Hasbro Children's Foundation

Charles Hayden Foundation

The William Randolph Hearst Foundation

Clarence E. Heller Charitable Foundation

The William and Flora Hewlett Foundation

The James Irvine Foundation

The Robert Wood Johnson Foundation

Walter S. Johnson Foundation

Ewing Marion Kauffman Foundation

W.K. Kellogg Foundation

John S. and James L. Knight Foundation

Lilly Endowment, Inc.

The MBK Foundation

Mr. and Mrs. Sanford N. McDonnell

The John D. and Catherine T. MacArthur Foundation

A.L. Mailman Family Foundation, Inc.

Charles Stewart Mott Foundation

National Institute on Drug Abuse (NIDA),
    National Institutes of Health

National Science Foundation

Nippon Life Insurance Foundation

Karen and Christopher Payne Foundation

The Pew Charitable Trusts

The Pinkerton Foundation

The Rockefeller Foundation

Louise and Claude Rosenberg, Jr. Family Foundation

The San Francisco Foundation

Shinnyo-En Foundation

Silver Giving Foundation

The Spencer Foundation

Spunk Fund, Inc.

Stuart Foundation

The Stupski Family Foundation

The Sulzberger Foundation, Inc.

Surdna Foundation, Inc.

John Templeton Foundation

U.S. Department of Education

Wallace-Reader's Digest Funds

Wells Fargo Bank

Caring School Community™
Reorder Information

Classroom Packages

Each grade-level package contains a Class Meetings Kit (grades K–1 or 2–6), Teacher's Calendar (grades K–1 or 2–6), *Cross-Age Buddies Activity Book, Homeside Activities* (grade specific), and *Schoolwide Community-Building Activities.*

Kindergarten Classroom Package	CSCK00
Grade 1 Classroom Package	CSC100
Grade 2 Classroom Package	CSC200
Grade 3 Classroom Package	CSC300
Grade 4 Classroom Package	CSC400
Grade 5 Classroom Package	CSC500
Grade 6 Classroom Package	CSC600

Classroom Packages with Read-Aloud Values Library

Kindergarten Classroom Package with Library (10 titles)	CSCKLK
Grade 1 Classroom Package with Library (10 titles)	CSCKL1
Grade 2 Classroom Package with Library (10 titles)	CSCKL2
Grade 3 Classroom Package with Library (10 titles)	CSCKL3
Grade 4 Classroom Package with Library (10 titles)	CSCKL4
Grade 5 Classroom Package with Library (10 titles)	CSCKL5
Grade 6 Classroom Package with Library (9 titles)	CSCKL6
Complete Read-Aloud Values Library (69 titles)	CSCL00

Principal's Package   CSCP00

Each package contains Class Meetings Kits (grades K–1 and 2–6), Teacher's Calendars (grades K–1 and 2–6), *Cross-Age Buddies Activity Book, Homeside Activities* (grades K–6), *Schoolwide Community-Building Activities, Principal's Leadership Guide,* Principal's Calendar, Implementation Schedule, and Observation Forms.

Available separately

Class Meeting Lessons Package K–1 (contains Class Meeting Lessons K–1 and Teacher's Calendar)	CMLP00
Class Meeting Lessons Package 2–6 (contains Class Meeting Lessons 2–6 and Teacher's Calendar)	CMLP20
Cross-Age Buddies Activities Book	BAB000
Schoolwide Community-Building Activities	SAB000
Homeside Activities: Kindergarten	HABK00
Homeside Activities: Grade One	HAB100
Homeside Activities: Grade Two	HAB200
Homeside Activities: Grade Three	HAB300
Homeside Activities: Grade Four	HAB400
Homeside Activities: Grade Five	HAB500
Homeside Activities: Grade Six	HAB600
Principal's Leadership Guide	CSCPLG
Principal's Observation Forms	CSCPOF

Ordering Information:
To order call 800.666.7270 * fax 510.842.0348 * log on to www.devstu.org * e-mail pubs@devstu.org

Or Mail Your Order to:
Developmental Studies Center * Publications Department * 2000 Embarcadero, Suite 305 * Oakland, CA 94606

DEVELOPMENTAL STUDIES CENTER™